I0618388

LANDSCAPES OF FRANCE

LANDSCAPES OF FRANCE

PAINTED BY THE MASTERS

Andrew Heritage

CHARTWELL BOOKS, INC.

First published in Great Britain in 1988 by
Octopus Books Limited
Michelin House
81 Fulham Road, London SW3 6RB

This 1988 edition
Published by

CHARTWELL BOOKS, INC.
A Division of **BOOK SALES, INC.**
110 Enterprise Avenue,
Secaucus, New Jersey 07094

ISBN 1-55521-194-1

Editor: Marilyn Inglis
Art Editor: Lisa Tai
Designer: Behram Kapadia
Picture Researcher: Gale Carlill
Production Controller: Garry Lewis
Indexer: Ella Skene

Typeset by Tradespools Ltd, Frome, Somerset
Printed in Hong Kong

Jacket illustration: The Pond at St C... (c. 1895)
by Jean-Léon Gérôme (Richard Green Collection, London).
Title page: Four Poplars (1891) by Claude Monet
(The Metropolitan Museum of Art, New York).

CONTENTS

Foreword 6

The History of a Landscape 8

Paris 30

South of Paris 50

North of Paris 62

Rivers 74

The Mountains 86

Normandy 96

Brittany and Biscay 112

Provence 126

The Mediterranean Coast 140

Biographical Notes on the Artists 154

Index 172

FOREWORD

All landscapes are the product of their history and that of the people who inhabit them. In the developed countries, especially those of Europe, the landscape can be read like an historical document, a living record of the past. The landscape of each country is unique and sometimes immediately recognizable – it is often emblematic, embodying at a fundamental level, certain characteristics which we might call national.

The theme of this book is to evaluate the landscape of France as it has been interpreted by its painters. Any survey of this kind must at the outset deal with two problems; the variety of the French landscape, and the surprising absence of a domestic French landscape painting tradition until the last 150 years. The topography of France itself, encompassing as it does a great variety of landscapes, is not as easily typified as, say, the mountains of Switzerland or the flat expanses of the Netherlands. Therefore we must look at how the landscape we can see today evolved – identify the geological, historical and cultural processes which have sculpted its modern face – and also try to assess the kind of landscapes which confronted those who have painted it in the past. Only then can we make sense of the story of landscape painting in France.

The following chapters have been arranged in order to place the major developments of French landscape painting in a basic historical sequence. Naturally, certain painters moved around France throughout their careers, and their work may appear out of sequence. This is not, however, a list of biographical notes – it is the relationship between the artist and the landscape about him which remains our primary concern.

A number of people offered advice and help, and without them this book would not exist; David Sawyer, Ulrich Finke, Judy Martin and Marilyn Inglis all have my thanks. But above all, this book is dedicated to my wife, Ailsa, and to George.

ALFRED SISLEY
FLOODS AT PORT-MARLY,
1876
Louvre, Paris

THE HISTORY OF A LANDSCAPE

During the last Ice Age, some 20,000 years ago, the glaciers of the enlarged northern ice cap failed to reach France. The landscape there is thus free from their sculpting effect and from the anomalous geological deposits they left as they retreated which characterize the landscapes of France's neighbours in northern Europe. The French landmass is formed by a group of rocky volcanic and sedimentary outcrops, which are separated by four large river systems. Comparisons between the modern borders of France and those of the Roman province of Gaul in the first century AD or the Frankish empire of Charlemagne at the turn of the eighth century AD are revealing; the geographical configuration of France seems to have altered little over the last 2000 years. This observation, as we shall see, belies the truth, but it has some relevance, as France enjoys a number of natural boundaries. The country is bounded to the south-west by the great mountain chain of the Pyrenees and to the east by the Jura mountains and the Alps. These formidable natural barriers are linked in the south by a 300-mile (483-km) stretch of often inhospitable Mediterranean coast. To the west, running northwards from the Pyrenees, is the Atlantic shoreline, a 1000-mile (1609-km) stretch of sandy, windswept beaches encompassing the coast of the Bay of Biscay and the Channel, broken midway by the massive craggy outcrop of the Breton peninsula. In the north-east the steep, wooded valleys of the Rhine, Saar and Moselle river systems link the Jura mountains with the forested bulks of the Vosges, Eifel and Ardennes mountains. It is only in the extreme north that the natural limits of the country become less clearly defined. Here, open plains roll northwards to Flanders and the Low Countries, a tract of terrain scarred by centuries of warfare; an inviting passage for invasion, it was exploited from the earliest times by barbarian hordes, and formed the corridor through which France was invaded three times over the last 120 years.

Within these broad natural confines France comprises over half a million square miles (over a million square kilometres) of territory, encompassing hugely contrasting topographical regions: the undulating northern plains of Artois and Picardy give way to the gentle river valleys of the Oise, the Marne, the Aisne, the Aube and the Yonne which rise in the uplands of Champagne and Burgundy and converge on the Seine near Paris, flowing westwards to the fertile fields of Normandy. To the south the broad, wooded tract of Fontainebleau looks down to the basin of the river Loire, the seat of the medieval French ruling classes, its northerly tributaries picking their way through the domains of Blois and Vendôme, the southerly branches enriching the plains of Berry and Poitou.

The Massif Central provides a huge, crenellated

THE LIMBOURG BROTHERS
SEPTEMBER FROM "LES TRÈS RICHES HEURES", PAINTED FOR THE DUKE OF BERRY,
1413–16
Condé Museum, Chantilly

mountain range which divides the landmass, its steep flanks incised to the west by the rivers Dordogne and Lot. Here, in the caves and deep defiles, some of the earliest European human remains have been found. To the south-west these heights look over the gentler valleys of Aveyron and further to the rich, warm plains of Guyenne, Gascony and the river Garonne. To the southeast the harsher terrain of Languedoc leads down to the alternately dry and marshy Mediterranean coast. Between the Massif Central and the foothills of the Alps rises the culturally and agriculturally rich corridor of the Rhône valley, the traditional passageway from the lands of the western Mediterranean to the countries of the north-western seaboard, first used by the Celts and ancient Greek colonists and in the Middle Ages providing France with a source of huge revenues from the flow of commerce.

Across this broad physical canvas lie the indelible marks made by the human inhabitants who have shaped the landscape in which they live. Although the political vicissitudes of France since the days of Charlemagne are complex, the actual face of the landscape has a simpler story. The region emerged from the Dark Ages clothed in heavy forest. Many of the villages, towns and roads of Roman Gaul and of Charlemagne's time had been destroyed, and cultivated land had reverted to waste. Vikings had caused massive depopulation in Normandy, and the ancient ports of the Mediterranean were prey to Arab raiders. Finally, a huge incursion of marauding Hungarian Magyars had swept across the French heartland, wasting towns, villages and farms in their path.

The reunification of France in the Middle Ages was dominated by the struggle with England for control of the Angevin kingdom of western France. Following England's conquest of Normandy in 1204, English possessions in south-west France were reduced and by 1260 were limited to the areas of Perigord, Guyenne and Gascony. The north of France too was under the intermittent control of England and Burgundy, and the English were not finally expelled from French soil (with the exception of Calais) until 1453. The ultimate goals of this struggle were economic; western France supported dairy farming and a wide range of crops including wheat, barley, rye, oats and sorghum. More significantly, however, control of the increasingly densely populated areas of the Ile de France, Normandy, Picardy, Artois and Flanders meant control of many trade routes to northern Europe and Scandinavia, and of the wool and linen textile industry which was developing there. Although the French throne finally achieved control, the effect of continuing warfare was expensive: a powerful, knightly aristocracy with a complex feudal system of labour dues, taxation and personal services was perpetuated, and although many French peasants established a share-cropping arrangement (*métayage*) with their overlords, it was not until the Revolution in 1789 that this antiquated and repressive system was finally demolished.

The landscape of rural France still shows the effect of this. The village-based economy of small fields and limited, near-subsistence cropping became firmly entrenched. Unlike British and Dutch farmers the French

NICOLAS POUSSIN
THE BURIAL OF PHOCION (DETAIL), 1648
The Earl of Derby, Knowsley, Lancashire

did not respond to the challenge of increasing production quotas and diversifying crops and farming methods, developments which signalled the end of feudal farming patterns, nor to the emergence of more scientific and economic agricultural methods which led to larger field patterns, the reduction of livestock in favour of cash-cropping and the ruthless clearing of land for tillage. Britain and the Netherlands bear the least forest per acre of any countries in Europe. France, until the formation of the EEC, largely escaped these excesses. The traditional nature of rural life in France remained unchanged in many areas until the twentieth century. This is reflected in the survival today of regional lore and folk tradition in Alsace, Brittany, Languedoc and Provence.

The process of recovery focused, from about AD 1000, around monastic communities at centres such as St Denis near Paris, Auxerre, Vezelay and Cluny, and around the scattered castles of powerful ley-lords. The forest was gradually cleared, feudal agricultural communities were founded, and eventually a series of major fairs emerged in the Ile de France and Champagne, among the most important being Provins, Troyes, Bar-Sur-Aube and Lagny, which straddled the routes from Flanders and the Channel to the Rhône valley, the Alpine passes and Italy.

The pattern of village-based agriculture which was to dominate the French landscape had been established, and the traditional seat of French power, around Paris and the Ile de France, came into focus. The establishment of new towns (*villeneuves*) and regional centres by French kings such as Louis VI (1108–37) and Louis VII (1137–80) was seen as a means of consolidating political control, but as more and more land came under the plough many regional centres acquired an independent wealth and influence often based on annual fairs which they have never relinquished: the Gothic cathedral towers of Beauvais, Chartres, Rheims and Bourges still dominate the surrounding landscape. Lyons, due to its contacts with Italy and Germany, was the financial capital of France for most of the fifteenth and sixteenth centuries. Marseilles thrived on its command of Mediterranean trade. Beaucaire, on the Rhône, hosted a number of major exchange fairs, and Nîmes conducted a lucrative textile trade with Spain. Moreover, the continuing political power of separate regions such as Burgundy meant that when, by the beginning of the sixteenth century, they were finally absorbed into France, they retained a strong sense of regional autonomy.

The extension of French royal power over the whole country took several centuries, and can be traced in the pattern of castle building. The fortified early medieval castles in Blois and the Loire valley soon gave way to a more decorative and elaborate style of palace and château, surrounded by parkland and hunting grounds, with villages neatly tucked away behind trees. The gentle valley of the Loire basin encouraged an agricultural pattern which comprised broad cultivated valley floors, a mixture of root-crop cultivation and grazing on hilltops, and coppicing – the maintenance of woodland for fuel and building materials – along the steeper shoulders of the hills and ridges. This pattern can still be seen today in the Loire valley.

Where medieval royal power was less secure the landscape bears less peacefully domestic traces. The Arabs had been expelled from the Mediterranean coast of France by AD 972 and the ports of Narbonne, Fraxinetum (Frainet) and Marseilles were secured and fortified. By the mid-twelfth century, they attracted shipping trade with the dominant Italian markets of Genoa and Pisa. Here the massive walls of the fortress port of Aigues Mortes seem to grow out of the rocky barren coast. The south, or Midi, was the setting for a dramatic revolt against the centralising monarchy, based in the city of Albi. The adherence of the Albigensians to a heretical form of Christianity – Catharism – provided the monarchy with an excuse to launch a crusade against them, led by Simon de Montfort, which culminated with the bloody siege of the great medieval fortress at Carcassone in 1209.

With the expulsion of the English, the centre of French political power became firmly established in the Ile de France. Paris had emerged from the Dark Ages as one of the most populous cities of Europe. It soon became one of the most powerful, and a major political and cultural centre. Francis I (1494–1547) was to launch the city on to the international Renaissance scene when the foundations of an ambitious palace complex were laid to the south of the city, at Fontainebleau. He imported sculptors, architects, and artists from Italy to decorate the palace. Around this hub revolved the aristocratic courtly life of the sixteenth century. A massive expanse of forest in the region was set aside as a hunting park and still remains today, now a huge recreation area for the people of Paris.

The final stage in the consolidation of the French state was reached in the seventeenth century, during the reign of Louis XIV (1638–1715). A series of treaties and wars finally established the frontier in the north and northeast. These gains were secured by the construction of a *barrière de fer*, a string of forts along all the borders of France. Although Louis' wars were immensely costly, causing high taxation and undermining to some extent the growth of the French economy, the centralized state which he established in turn helped to stimulate the

▲ JEAN ANTOINE WATTEAU
LE BAL CHAMPÊTRE, c.1715
Coll. Viscomte de Neailles, Paris

CLAUDE LORRAINE
ASCANIUS AND THE STAG, 1682
Ashmolean Museum, Oxford

exploitation of France's enormous resources and did much to transform the landscape. The most significant of those resources was the population, estimated in 1700 at 20 million, which was concentrated in the north, the northeast and along the Mediterranean coast. There was a spate of road and canal building, linking several hitherto isolated regions. Trade and production of wine, cloth, glass, paper and iron brought wealth and expansion to regional centres such as Nancy and Lyons, and to the bustling entrepôts of Toulon, Marseilles, Bordeaux, La Rochelle, St Malo, Dieppe, Boulogne and Calais. At this time the creation of new cultivable land accelerated. On the one hand, the consumption of standing forest by new industries for paper and for building, especially shipbuilding, led to an increase in agricultural acreage. On the other, major land reclamation schemes were encouraged, especially on the Landes coast west of Bordeaux and in certain marshy regions on the Mediterranean littoral.

France had become the most powerful state in Europe, and that power was reflected in the great baroque architectural schemes and gardens which dominated

Paris and in the final stage of château-building around Paris and in the Loire valley. It was exemplified, however, by the extension of a royal hunting lodge at Versailles into the greatest palace complex in Europe. Its structure reflects the contemporary French attitude to nature and the landscape. The visitor proceeds from the massive but ordered classical grandeur of the palace itself to formal terraces and parterres – orange gardens, miniature trees, low box hedges and decorative flower beds set into intricate geometric patterns and gravelled pathways. From these extends a dynamic sweeping perspective of water gardens, lawns, fountains and statuary. Proceeding along this axis, the visitor is tempted to investigate lateral vistas, avenues of mature broad-leafed trees receding to elaborate focal points – yet more statues, fountains, summerhouses and architectural follies which seemingly perch on the cusp between the ordered, man-made Eden and the wilderness beyond. The whole complex occupies 250 acres (101 hectares), and represents Renaissance man's moulding of nature to his will. The landscape was to be ordered and dominated, rather than enjoyed in the raw.

During the eighteenth century the focus of French society shifted from the courtly aristocracy towards the entrepreneurial landowning and industrial middle classes. Regional towns and cities were embellished by local worthies (some, such as Nancy, were substantially rebuilt) and parks and gardens were set aside for the enjoyment of nature domesticated. In the countryside, however, it was not until the Revolution of 1789 that the wind of change began to blow. Extensive agrarian peasant revolts, culminating in the Great Fear uprising of 1789, caused massive food shortages in the cities – one of the major factors in the outbreak of urban riots in Paris and other centres. Feudalism was finally destroyed. In northern France and Guyenne field sizes gradually increased and the countryside there began to take on the features of more modern agricultural techniques. The political chaos of the Directoire and the Napoleonic empire held back the process of economic development, but by 1850 a new revolution, in industry, was making its mark. The construction of the French railway network was under way, to be largely completed by 1870. This, and the building of new canals linking the natural waterways, opened up many rural areas. The mining of coal and iron began on a large scale in Lorraine, Brittany and Maine, in the foothills of the Alps and Pyrenees, and in the Massif Central. A new kind of regional centre based on heavy industry sprang up. As elsewhere in Europe, the population left the countryside in droves following the promise of more lucrative work in the towns and cities.

The novels of Balzac neatly characterize the middle-class society of wealthy provincial towns with industrial economies at the beginning of the period. The novels of Zola paint a bleaker picture of the fate of the industrial urban proletariat by the end of the century.

One aspect of industrialization which not only irrevocably changed certain areas of France, but which also changed people's attitudes towards the countryside, was the ability to travel. With trains, bicycles and eventually automobiles the urban population could easily and cheaply visit the countryside for recreation. Spa towns in the Alps and the sandy areas of the coast became fashionable. Normandy was easily accessible from Paris, and the ports and fishing harbours there rapidly adapted to their new role as resorts. Slightly later, by the turn of the nineteenth century, the Biscay coast and the Côte d'Azur became the places to visit during the French holiday month, August. The sleepy Mediterranean villages were transformed into playgrounds for the rich. The impact of relatively cheap travel extended beyond the national borders of France; Paris had a reputation as the cultural centre of Europe which dated back nearly 200 years to the reign of Louis XIV. This image acquired cult status in the nineteenth century, when the capital became the prime target on the transatlantic tourists' itinerary. The gutting and replanning of Paris served to re-launch the city as the foremost modern capital of Europe.

The impact of tourism on the French landscape was, however, considerably outweighed by the appalling effects on it of modern warfare. The French suffered a foretaste of this when the Prussians invaded in 1871. Even this was minor compared to the devastation wrought by the Great War, however. Over four years from 1914 the villages and towns of the Western Front, a broad band of land running from the North Sea coast to the Rhine, were simply obliterated and field patterns, hedges, lanes and woods were pulverized into a quagmire of mud and metal. The extensive undermining of enemy trench-works only underscored the damage caused by lengthy periods of heavy artillery bombardment and almost continual mortar fire. The German shelling of Verdun in 1916 quite literally vaporized all the topsoil in the region, and even today, 70 years later, the land has not recovered. Although most of the battlefields of the Western Front were reclaimed by the plough in the inter-war years the traces of the historical landscape were

HUBERT ROBERT
THE OLD BRIDGE
National Gallery of Art, Washington

utterly erased, to be replaced by a scarification of trenches and earthworks.

The various phases of the Allied invasion of Normandy some 30 years later, preceded by enormous bombardments, this time from the sea and air, had a similar effect. It is difficult today to travel from Caen to Cherbourg and find a building or monument which is more than 30 years old, or which has not been substantially rebuilt.

In the last 40 years the face of France has, of course, altered more rapidly than at any time in its past. The financial aid and concessions and cropping policies introduced by the European Economic Community have now radically altered the face of French agriculture, and thus that of the modern landscape of France. The enlargement of fields with the attendant destruction of hedgerows and woodland, the absorption of small family farms by larger, business-oriented conglomerates, and the ruthless equation whereby large-scale 'prairie' farming brings large-scale investment returns have begun to alter irretrievably the rural balance. Furthermore, the development of commuting has created ever-widening rings around major towns and cities within which the truly rural population has declined to make way for wealthier people who can afford to travel considerable distances to work while still enjoying the benefits of country life. The gentrification of rural farmhouses and cottages has occurred on a large scale, and the relatively lax building laws over the past 100 years or so have led to the widespread erection of new houses outside towns and villages, gradually spreading domestic habitation into hitherto unoccupied areas.

Finally, tourism in recent years has again altered the economic balance of specific regions. The popularity of skiing has brought sudden wealth to many Alpine villages, significantly disrupting the local economies and landscape. The coasts of Normandy and Biscay are less popular with sun-seeking foreign tourists, although they remain favourites with the French themselves. The Mediterranean coast has borne the brunt of the kind of urban and commercial development associated with mass tourism. It is difficult today to pick out the quiet harbours painted by Cézanne and Matisse from the esplanades and high-rise blocks of the Côte d'Azur. Certain areas of rural France, especially Perigord and the Dordogne, have also enjoyed a significant change in their economy; here the attraction of a cheap, isolated second home or retirement retreat has caused an influx of foreign settlers and money, and many French farmers lease holiday accommodation.

So it can be seen how, over the centuries, the French landscape has been altered and adapted by human intervention. Despite political and economic advances

LOUIS GABRIEL MOREAU
THE HILLS OF MENTON
Louvre, Paris

the rural farming society remained undeveloped for several centuries, and the more remote regions managed to retain unique characteristics until very recently. On the other hand, the urban section of late medieval and early modern French society evolved a taste for a domesticated rural idyll of parks and gardens. Fortunately for us, much can still be enjoyed today.

Painting the French landscape

The landscape stands with the human figure and the devotional image as one of the three major motifs of world art. Like figure painting, it is primarily the product of the artist painting the world he sees about him. Unlike figure painting and religious iconography, representation of the landscape is, for the most part, confined to graphic art, and it only developed where drawing and painting became sufficiently sophisticated. China, Japan and Korea all produced distinctive and refined historical traditions of landscape painting.

In modern European art the landscape was a late starter, even more so in France, where a true native genre did not emerge until the nineteenth century. To understand why this happened, and the circumstances under which most of the paintings in this book were conceived, we must look briefly at the development of landscape painting in Europe as a whole.

Landscape was a popular theme among Egyptian, Hellenistic and classical Roman painters. The latter mastered one of the fundamental problems of the genre – the creation of the illusion of space – and the rediscovery of Roman works, especially decorations and wall paintings, was to provide considerable stimulus to their European descendants. Something of the artistry of the original Roman landscapists (many of whom were in fact itinerant Greek painters) was preserved by the artists employed at the Byzantine court and their contemporaries under the patronage of the Holy Roman Emperors Charlemagne (742–814) and Otto I (912–73). Illuminated manuscripts produced during their reigns, such as the Utrecht Psalter (c. 816–35), often contain scenes in which figures are arranged in landscape settings; although fairly rudimentary, the technique used to create the illusion of space and depth shows that classical learning had not been completely forgotten.

During the later Middle Ages, the representation of landscape was used as a foil for the organization of the figures which were the real subject of the paintings – landscapes merely solved the problem of what to do with the background of a historical, religious or narrative subject. In the Gothic style of art which became popular north of the Alps during the early and high Middle Ages this problem was often bypassed: a plain coloured backdrop, or a flattened architectural setting for figures occupying a shallow foreground space, were common solutions. During the fourteenth century, however, landscape backdrops became increasingly popular. Using intense colours and an imaginative combination of forms, artists created that style which is identified with the great feudal courts of medieval Europe and is known as International Gothic. Their subject matter was either devotional or took its themes from the literary and courtly life which is associated with Chaucer and with the troubadours of southern France.

The first great instance of French landscape painting is to be found in the illuminated pages of *Les Belles Heures* and *Les Très Riches Heures*, painted for the Duke of Berry (1413–16). Illustrated devotional calendars had occurred in early medieval manuscript illumination, but in a much more limited form; classical painters, too, had shown the cycle of the seasons. These pages, however, richly decorated by the three Limbourg brothers, Pol, Hennequin and Herman, create convincing and delicately detailed views of contemporary courtly and rural life set in carefully observed landscapes; each page represents the landscape and the principal pursuits of a month of the year. While the wealth of observation in these books is uniquely their own, the intricacy of detail may be partly attributed to the Limbourg brothers' training as goldsmiths. The feel for rendering spatial values, however, may have been the result of a visit to Italy.

The incorporation of an observed and identifiable landscape into figure painting had first occurred in Italy. Sometimes the setting reflected the subject: Lorenzetti's *Allegory of Good and Bad Government* (1338), a fresco for Siena Town Hall (the Palazzo Publico) recreates identifiable buildings in Siena itself and includes generalized treatments of features from the surrounding countryside. Later, Italian Renaissance painters such as Piero della Francesca would set historical and religious subjects such as the *Baptism of Christ* (c. 1440–50) in a clearly observed setting of Tuscan cypress trees and olive groves.

It was an artist of the next generation who, although he never painted a pure landscape, realized the full potential of landscape as a motif in figure painting. Leonardo da Vinci left numerous sketches of topography and natural phenomena such as waterfalls, storms and geological formations in his notebooks, and he used these observations to construct dynamic imaginary landscape

RICHARD PARKES BONINGTON
THE PARK AT VERSAILLES, c.1826
Louvre, Paris

VICTOR HUGO
THE CHÂTEAU AT VIANDEN, 1871
Maison de Victor Hugo, Paris

◀ EUGÈNE DELACROIX
STILL LIFE WITH LOBSTER, 1827
Louvre, Paris

backdrops in paintings such as *The Virgin of the Rocks* (c. 1483–85) and *Mona Lisa* (c. 1503–6). These background views are not meant to be real, but part of the poetic world which the artist has created – an aspect of the inner life of the figures in the painting.

Leonardo spent the last three years of his life in France, at the invitation of Francis I. Here, and in the Netherlands, later fifteenth-century painters such as Campin, the Van Eycks and Rogier van der Weyden devoted increasingly substantial areas of their paintings to the representation of landscape. They introduced greater naturalism into the International Gothic style; figures still occupied a limited foreground space, often defined by elaborate architectural frameworks, but which begin to give way through windows or doors on to extensive landscape vistas. These painters largely ignored the accurate perspective construction espoused by their Italian contemporaries in favour of an instinctive aerial perspective established by the juxtaposition and modulation of receding scale and intense colours. Although many features of these landscapes are self-evidently observed (especially some of van der Weyden's townscapes), the final effect is not topographic, but symbolic. Every feature has a specific symbolic meaning, not least the contrived and compressed landscape.

The first modern European landscapes, paintings of views without any other subject and, most significantly, without a story, can be attributed to the German artist Altdorfer. Many of his watercolours and etchings are pure landscape, and even in certain figure subjects such as *St George and the Dragon* (c. 1505–10) or *The Battle of the Issus* (1529) the landscape utterly overwhelms the tiny figures. It is no accident that he painted in Munich, located midway between the Netherlands and Italy. He was one of the first artists to combine the achievements and qualities of the two regional traditions.

By the beginning of the sixteenth century the final stages of the political unification of France had been reached, and the nation had become the most powerful and wealthy state in Europe. Francis I (1494–1547) was an active patron of the arts, and his palace at Fontainebleau was conceived as a direct challenge to the cultural hegemony of the wealthy humanist princes who ruled the city states of Italy. For the decoration of his new palace, in the absence of appropriate native expertise, Francis invited various Italian masters, such as Rosso and Primaticcio, to plan and supervise the work. They were aided by French and Flemish journeymen, and a unique style of art and decoration was developed which combined Flemish colouring with Italian classical form, decorative flair with intimate sensuousness. As with most art of the period, known as Mannerist, the effect was both eclectic and inventive.

The principal pictorial subjects were themes drawn from classical mythology, played out by elegant nudes set in artificial architectural schemes and ornate stucco work, or in equally artificial 'classical' landscape settings. The latter tended to follow set formulae developed in Italy – visions of an Arcadian countryside scattered with classical architectural fragments, with distant mountains, receding rivers or coastlines, and idealized trees used as foreground and middle ground framing elements. The effect was highly contrived and composed.

The work on the palace continued under Francis' sons Henry II and Charles IX. When Primaticcio was joined in 1552 by Niccolò dell'Abbate a more mature style of classical landscape appeared. Much of their work at Fontainebleau has been overpainted, but Niccolò executed several large canvases for Charles IX, including *Orpheus and Eurydice* (1557). Although ostensibly a mythological subject, the figures are minute, the real content of the painting being an extensive view of an idealized, idyllic Mediterranean shoreline reaching away to a distant horizon, the coast dotted with an improbable mixture of buildings. The landscape is a homogenous whole, and relies on a Flemish freshness of colour and a panoramic vista which beckons with poetic possibilities.

Niccolò's work prefaced the development of a long tradition of classical landscape painting in France, which coalesced around the figures of Poussin and Claude.

Despite, or possibly because of, the Fontainebleau schools, Italy continued to exert a constant pull. A steady stream of painters from northern Europe began to cross the Alps to train in the workshops of major artists. In many, such as that of Annibale Carracci, they would be encouraged to sketch the world about them, to exercise the eye, to master the representation of objects and views with ease and fluency, abilities which would eventually aid imaginative invention; but the final aim of their training would be the production of large-scale religious, classical and mythological subjects for both serious and decorative settings. (Significantly, it was Carracci who produced the first masterpiece of modern classical landscape in his *Flight into Egypt* (1603).)

The kind of visual and graphic virtuosity encouraged by Mannerist and Baroque painters did not always produce the desired results. Some of the most charming French landscape studies of the seventeenth century came from the pen of the prolific maverick Jacques Callot (c. 1592–1635). A kind of visual journalist, he prefigured in many ways the 'painters of modern life' of the nineteenth century. Born in Nancy, he trained in Rome and Florence and acquired a Mannerist fluency of line and a taste for the grotesque. Callot's representations of low-life figures, of beggars and fairs, enjoyed great popularity in the court of Louis XIII. His enormous oeuvre includes many delicate landscape studies, presumably observed in his native Lorraine, but not specifically located or identifiable. These were worked up into small etchings or incorporated into the backgrounds of, for example, *Les Grands Misères de la Guerre* (1633–35), a series of scenes from the Thirty Years' War.

However, it was with the classical landscape that the main strand of development continued, in the careers of the two first masters of French landscape painting, Nicolas Poussin (1593/4–1665) and Claude Lorraine (1600–82). They both, ironically, spent most of their working lives in Italy. Possibly they had seen the work of Niccolò dell'Abbate; certainly they were aware of Italian classical landscape painting, and both ultimately belong to the Roman Baroque school; but their influence on French painting was enormous.

Poussin trained in Paris, in a cultural atmosphere increasingly flavoured by a Catholic taste for austere

EDOUARD MANET
DÉJEUNER SUR L'HERBE,
1863
Musée d'Orsay, Paris

classicism. By 1624 he was working in Rome, where the stimulation of direct contact with classical art and architecture and the vigorous intellectualism of the Counter-Reformation papacy combined to produce in his work a unique style. His formal achievement was in the creation of clearly modelled, dynamic and classically informed composition, initially in the organization of figure groups and architectural elements; soon this concern spread beyond the foreground features of his paintings and extended to a rigorous re-invention of the classical landscape itself. In Poussin's hands the genre was transformed from a largely formulaic manner of creating an idyllic and fantastic ambience into an exposition of the moral and philosophical themes of his subject matter. Much of this was achieved by his meticulous attention to archaeological detail and a careful interpretation of a multiplicity of literary sources. Poussin's approach, widely emulated and often debased, formed a fundamental principle in French art – an ideological core in the teachings of the Académie des Beaux-Arts (established by Louis XIV's minister Colbert in 1663, and the first such academy in northern Europe; the French Academy in Rome was founded in 1666). Poussin's influence resurfaced during the Neo-classical revival at the end of the eighteenth century (especially in the work of David) and was to inform and perplex even Cézanne, Matisse, Masson and Picasso.

The work of Claude Lorraine is less intellectually

demanding, and has always enjoyed an enormous popular appeal. He worked in Italy from the age of 12, first in Naples and then in Rome, where the surrounding countryside of the *campagna* and the Alban Hills provided him with a great source of inspiration. Where Poussin's view of the classical Roman world was concerned with Stoic philosophers and Republican virtues (presented as mirrors and examples for his contemporaries), Claude was fascinated by the nostalgic qualities of the pre-Republican, mythical Golden Age, and with the poetic world of Virgil. Where Poussin's work was informed by archaeological and philosophical erudition, Claude's imaginary world was derived from classical poetry and a close observation of the contemporary landscape of the Roman *campagna* (which, even today, bears numerous evocative traces of the ancient past). Stylistically, where Poussin's paintings were welded together by a firm, clear compositional structure, Claude's compositions were more intuitive, the poetic vision of the paintings unified by a delicate control of colour and a suffusion of light.

The combined achievements of these two masters formed basic teaching models at the Académie des Beaux-Arts, which extolled classicism as the one source of serious artistic endeavour and promulgated this assertion in rigorous artistic training and working

EDOUARD MANET
MONET IN HIS FLOATING STUDIO, 1874
Bayerische Staatssammlung, Munich

methods. A tradition became established whereby French landscape painters could only seek suitable subjects south of the Alps.

In the early years of the eighteenth century the awareness of nature increased. This can partly be attributed to the growth of natural sciences at the time, although these initially tended to reinforce the Renaissance notion that nature was there to be dominated by humanity. Where Louis XIV's palace of Versailles remains a supreme formal example of this tendency, many of the paintings of the following century reflect the less formal approach to nature manifested in the contemporary creation of urban gardens and carefully tended parks. The *fêtes champêtres*, picnics and bucolic games so delightfully described in the works of Watteau and Fragonard are shown taking place in parks and landscaped gardens. The paintings, although often full of the luxuriance of nature, rarely present extensive views; they are keyholes for voyeuristic glimpses of the leisured classes at dalliance and play. An exception which proves the rule is the masterpiece of the genre, Watteau's *Return from Cythera* (1717), a kind of hybrid between the imagined classical world of Claude and an imagined contemporary world of the Luxembourg Gardens.

By the end of the eighteenth century a profound revival in classical learning and emulation was under way, but still there is little trace of an indigenous landscape painting tradition. Rarified views of Parisian parks and boulevards are few in number, 'are often painted by foreign visitors (such as Kleyn) and remain informed by a classical outlook – contemporary France presented in the same manner as Rome.

At this point it is worth taking a step sideways, for by the turn of the eighteenth century both England and the Netherlands had well-established native landscape painting traditions. A comparison of the cultural ambience, of common ground and contrasts between France and her neighbours, reveals some reasons for this. During the Reformation in the sixteenth century, both the Netherlands and England had become Protestant countries while France retained her allegiance to Rome. Thus one might expect to see a decline in high religious art in the former countries; this was true, but a great number of works of art in eighteenth-century France were also secular in origin and purpose. Historical painting, portraiture and genre painting were popular in all three nations, and both France and the Netherlands developed the formal still life, in different ways, to a sophisticated degree. However, there was a fundamental difference in the way these nations viewed their countryside. In the Netherlands it was a highly prized resource, reclaimed at great cost from the sea and fought for at even greater cost between 1566 and 1648, when the Spanish finally conceded Dutch independence. The source of the new Republic's wealth was twofold – her rich agricultural land, and her increasingly substantial slice of global maritime trade. The recurring motifs of Dutch painting during the seventeenth and eighteenth centuries include trading ships, cultivated fields, fat, healthy livestock and agricultural and horticultural produce. Dutch art celebrated the nation's new-found religious and political freedom, tempered by the rapid growth of a modern agricultural and maritime economy operated by a wealthy middle class. The style of many of the paintings shows an almost scientific attention to detail, a pragmatism typical of a people who were busy inventing or improving clocks, chronometers, surveying instruments, agricultural implements, scientific and astronomical apparatus and insurance and banking systems.

This scientific approach was a major aspect too in English landscape painting, where a topographic tradition came to fruition in the eighteenth century. Similar, though less dramatic, economic, scientific and political changes were also occurring here. Native landscape painting, along with new agricultural techniques, began in emulation of the Dutch. By the mid-eighteenth century, paintings of the landscape, usually in watercolour, had come to be regarded as matters of personal record, and the selection of a suitably picturesque or sublime view a demonstration of personal taste. Personal wealth was often demonstrated by having a portrait painted in the sitter's own farm or parkland.

The topographic tradition was also linked to the English taste for travel, and the ability to turn out a competent watercolour view was regarded as an essential attribute of the educated person. Eventually this combination of topographic accuracy and demonstrative taste became increasingly elaborate, reaching a climax in the canvases of Constable (1776–1837) and Turner (1775–1851), elegiac and heroic hymns to nature in all her beauty, variety and power. The keynote to both their careers was the close observation of the flux and flow of nature – Constable's sketchbooks are filled with annotations on changing atmospheric conditions, colours and visibility. Turner, with typical grandiosity, had himself strapped to the mast of a ship during a heavy storm, the better to observe the effects of rain, wind and water. Both men produced endless quick on-the-spot sketches, shorthand impressions which would be used later to build up a major canvas in the studio. In their later years both would voice a preference for the immediacy and expressive qualities of these sketches, and to modern eyes they often seem superior to the finished, formal canvases. It is instructive to compare Constable's *Mill near Brighton*, painted at the beginning of the nineteenth century, with Van Gogh's *Moulin de la Galette*, painted in 1886. In subject they are similar, and to some extent in style; however, Constable's painting is the result of the direct observation of the scene before him, the nuances of colour, light and atmosphere noted down in a very spontaneous manner – but he would not have exhibited the picture formally. Van Gogh's work, again painted from nature, seems motivated also by personal forces, the impact of the image being seen as a major part of the final result. In the 50 or 60 years which divide the two pictures lies the great experience of French landscape painting.

Significantly, an exhibition of Constable's paintings in Paris in 1824 proved enormously popular and influential. The post-Revolutionary period in France had fostered a generation of Romantic philosophers, writers and artists. They were concerned with capturing emotional and emotive immediacy; the Romantic painters found the prevailing classical and historical school of painting too academic and dry for their tastes, so they began to develop a new approach to painting. Their subject matter was often contemporary, and self-consciously shocking, dealing with violent action and the human condition in extreme situations; their use of colour was unorthodox, and their paintings were calculated to give maximum visual effect – which often led them to be accused of a lack of preparation and finish. Nothing could be further from the truth, but the contrast between the work of the leaders of the school, Eugène Delacroix (1798–1863) and Théodore Géricault (1791–1824), and the cool elegance of the leading classical painter of the day, Dominique Ingres (1780–1867), is clear.

Although neither Delacroix nor Ingres produced major landscape paintings, Ingres painted some fine Italian studies early in his career. Géricault spent much of his short working life in England, where he saw the work of Constable and Turner. Delacroix too visited London, and enthused over the English landscape masters. *Still Life with Lobster* (1827) was an attempt by Delacroix to adapt their approach (a combination of topographic verisimilitude with a looser, more expressionistic application and selection of paint) to his own palette; elsewhere he often applied dabs or swirls of bright pure colour in a non-naturalistic fashion to create an overall visual effect of movement and dynamism. The effect worked extremely well, but it seems that Delacroix's interest in history painting and literary subjects precluded much attention to landscape in his later work.

Richard Parkes Bonington (c. 1801–28) was another English painter who helped to inspire a new interest in contemporary landscape painting in France. His bold use of a rich palette and loose modelling in the many paintings he executed in France brought him an enthusiastic public among the Romantics.

Thus can be seen two separate strands which come together at the exhibition of 1824; on the one hand a growing group of French Romantic writers and artists, keen to reject retrogressive modes and manners, in the arts as elsewhere, and eager to set out on a fresh, new appraisal of the world about them; on the other, the growing awareness in France of a long-standing and fruitful tradition of landscape painting developed by her northern European neighbours.

The subsequent development of French landscape painting is outlined in the following chapters of this book, and there is no need to go into great detail here. A progression of developments followed fairly neatly: a group of landscapists known as the Barbizon school began working, like Constable, Bonington and Turner, from nature, *en plein air*, during the 1830s and 1840s (see South of Paris chapter). Their style was an amalgam, showing traces of a standard classical training underlying their attempts to recreate directly in paint the vigour and splendour of nature in the wild.

Realism was a movement which grew out of some of the political preoccupations of Romanticism – the most outstanding of these being an awareness of social inequality and of urban and rural poverty. Realist landscape painters, such as Millet and Courbet (see South of Paris and Mountains chapters), evolved their style from that of the Barbizon group. They recognized that in order to convey unpleasant truths about society both style and presentation should be unquestionably true to nature and to life. The development of photography at the time provided an alternative means of expression, and to some extent was a threat to painting. The later works of the Realist movement began to assess the central problem of how to represent the subject accurately in paint, while moving beyond mere surface appearances.

Another development from Romanticism, linked to Realism, can be identified in the writings of the critic Charles Baudelaire. He was fascinated by the beauty of the contemporary (urban) world. In 1863 he advocated that the modern artist should turn his attention to the immediate world about him to observe fashions and street life, to attempt to capture movement and the fleeting impression – to become, in his words, 'The Painter of Modern Life'.

All of these trends – Romanticism, the Naturalism of the Barbizon painters, Realism and modernity – found a focal centre in adopting an anti-reactionary stance in the arts as much as in political and social life. In 1863, the same year as Baudelaire's essay was published, the French artistic establishment (still embodied in the

GEORGES SEURAT
LA GRANDE JATTE, 1884–86
Art Institute, Chicago

Académie des Beaux-Arts) was still advocating classicism and history painting; a confrontation with the new mood followed a heated controversy over the rejection of numerous impressive canvases submitted for the Académie's annual Salon. Surprisingly, the French monarch, Napoleon III, stepped in and arranged a *Salon des Refusés*, a decision which for many remains the point at which modern art came into existence.

The *Salon des Refusés* included works by Whistler, Pissarro and the young Cézanne, but the outstanding *succès de scandale* was Edouard Manet's *Déjeuner sur l'Herbe* (1863), a reinterpretation of a Renaissance composition – Titian's *Le Concert Champêtre* – in a modern setting. The notion of nudes set in a landscape was perfectly acceptable to the Académie, unless, as here, the setting was not classical but contemporary. The painting posed two formidable questions: for the Academician the question was 'Why should anyone wish to paint a group of bohemian contemporaries, of self-evidently loose morals, having a picnic?' For Manet and his admirers it was 'What have traditional, out-moded values got to offer us?' The answer to the latter was 'a lot' – but not in a fossilized state. Although the painting struck a substantial blow for modernism and opened the floodgates of modern art, few of the artists who enjoyed the freedom it established were unaware or unappreciative of the past.

The Impressionist painters had been working in a manner which sought to re-invent the art of painting, by concentrating on a careful analysis of light, colour and

PAUL CÉZANNE
LES GRANDES BAIGNEUSES,
1898–1905
Philadelphia Museum of Art

instantaneity, for several years before they were aware that they had formed a 'movement'. Their concerns represented a logical progression from Realism, and their subject matter (given their aims) was unavoidably modern in that they had to paint the world they saw about them. Thus landscapes were their most common motif.

By the time of the first Impressionist exhibition in 1874 it was clear that 'modern art' was here to stay. The founders of Impressionism tended to follow their original conceptions throughout their careers, none more so than Monet (see Paris, North of Paris and Normandy chapters). For younger artists, Impressionism was a solid platform from which to dive off into further developments; the platform which they saw in Impressionism was the re-invention of the act of painting itself. The dives, however, were into many different pools. Seurat and Signac devised a method of painting – called Divisionism – which purported to analyse light and colour more 'scientifically' than the Impressionists (see Paris and Normandy chapters). This consisted of applying paint in carefully controlled minuscule dabs or dots of colour – a style known as *pointilliste*. The exercise of such control led to a rather stolid and stilted effect, interpreted by many as a return to the pure forms of classicism. Cézanne (see North of Paris and Provence chapters) developed a unique modulation of Impressionist colour and constructive, patterned brushwork in order to imbue greater solidity to his canvases. For Gauguin and Van Gogh (see Brittany and Provence chapters), Impressionism provided an opportunity to use pure colours as expressive, rather than naturalistic, tools in a search for a means of conveying emotions, states of mind and other, more abstract notions. The variety of possibilities opened by the Impressionists was endless.

The following chapters present a regional survey of the various ways in which the French landscape has been painted. However, given the strange history of French landscape painting, the survey inevitably concentrates upon the golden age of modern painting between 1824 and the death of Cézanne in 1906.

NICOLAS DE STAËL
ROOFS, 1952
Musée National d'Art Moderne, Paris

PARIS

Paris is one of the great cities of Europe, today being the third largest with a population of 8.5 million and an area of 150 square miles (388 square kilometres) including the districts of Val de Marne, Seine St Denis and Hauts de Seine. Just after the last war these figures were 2.7 million and 41 square miles (106 square kilometres) respectively, indicating its rapid growth rate over the last 40 years. Anywhere else, this would mean that much of the older part of the city would be in danger of becoming overwhelmed by the sprawling mass of new development and suburbs and the problem of inner city decay would have set in with a vengeance. Fortunately this is not true of Paris; the survival of the city in all its parts, of the older sections within the new, is the result of considerable foresight in urban planning in the past and of a great sense of historical and cultural impetus. One aspect of that cultural impetus is its continuing reputation as a centre for the fine arts; it has to be said that Paris remains the most frequently painted city in the world.

Paris originated as a Gallic fishing settlement on the muddy Ile de la Cité, which provided a convenient bridging place on the broad and meandering river Seine. After Julius Caesar's conquest of central and northern Gaul in 56 BC the Romans established the more substantial fortified town of Lutetia Parisiorum on the site. The Seine then was navigable by ships well above Paris, and much of the city's early prosperity derived from control of river-borne trade and traffic. The Romans realized that the site formed a natural focal point for the routes from Aquitaine and Spain to northern and central Europe, and for routes from the Mediterranean to Britain and the North Sea. This feature has not altered through the centuries, and Paris remains at the heart of a network of communications, roads, railways and, latterly, motorways; these lines of communication do not pass through the city, but rather radiate from it.

The growth of Paris can be traced in more or less concentric rings, developing out from the Ile de la Cité. The Roman town spread initially to the left bank of the Seine (which bisects the modern city in a great arc), and continued to grow under the Merovingian and Frankish emperors. St Denis, traditionally the first bishop of Paris, was martyred on Montmartre (hence the name), and Ste Geneviève, the patron saint of the city, was said to have saved Paris by prayer from devastation at the hands of the Black Huns, although Attila's marauding hosts were in fact defeated by a combined Franco-Roman force at the battle of the Catalaunian Fields (AD 451), presumed to be in the vicinity of modern Troyes, some 80 miles away. Subsequent Germanic rulers, notably the Merovingians and Franks, made Paris their capital. Under

HUBERT ROBERT
DEMOLITION OF THE HOUSES ON PONT NOTRE-DAME, 1786
Musée Carnavalet, Paris

Hubert Robert here provides an interesting insight into the look of Paris at the most turbulent time in the history of the city. Immediately prior to the Revolution of 1789, major building works had been undertaken with a view to relieving the congested medieval streets at the heart of the city, in order to make the administration and control of the capital easier. It turned out that these measures were taken too late. Robert's view shows something of the dense, closely-packed housing which had built up over the centuries at the heart of the capital, spreading eventually even over the Seine bridges. The clearing of the slums and tenements at this time did little to relieve the problem of overcrowding and squalor, as the prime outcome of this period of development was the erection of a new city wall pierced by grandiose tax-collecting booths for levying tolls on incoming produce. It was very much this kind of economic pressure on the flow of goods from countries to towns which sparked off the bread riots which inaugurated the Revolution.

CHARLES MERYON
THE MORGUE, 1854
Victoria & Albert Museum, London

▶ JEAN BAPTISTE COROT
LE QUAI ORFEVRES, PARIS, 1833
Musée Carnavalet, Paris

Charlemagne (who established his own capital at Aachen over 200 miles (322 kilometres) to the north, now in Germany) the city became a centre of learning. During the mid-ninth century the settlement was razed by the Normans but swiftly recovered, was refortified, and successfully resisted further assaults later in the century.

Paris became confirmed as the capital of France when Hugh, Count of Paris and founder of the Capetian dynasty, was proclaimed king of France and Aquitaine in 987. He established the coronation as the eighth sacrament, thereby setting himself above all feudal lords and ensuring undisputed dynastic succession. From this point Paris expanded rapidly. Fortified walls were constructed by Philippe Auguste (1150-1223), enclosing some 600 acres (243 hectares). The University of Paris (Sorbonne) was founded in 1257 on the Left Bank, attracting a cluster of schools and colleges under its eaves, and their inhabitants' disputations laid the foundations of law and theology throughout Western Christendom. Paris rapidly became for western Europe what Constantinople was for the East – maybe not the undisputed political centre of its region but certainly the

▲ EDOUARD MANET
CONCERT IN THE TUILERIES GARDENS, 1862
National Gallery, London

EDOUARD MANET
PRELIMINARY STUDY FOR CONCERT IN THE TUILERIES GARDENS, c.1862
Private collection

CLAUDE MONET
THE CHURCH OF SAINT-GERMAIN L'AUXERROIS, PARIS, 1866
Nationalgalerie, Berlin

During the 1860s many of the urban Realists, especially of the younger generation, spurred on by Baudelaire's demands for 'Painters of Modern Life' turned their attention to the objective representation of life and events about them. Their work was largely devoid of the pathos and social comment found in the work of older Realists such as Millet, Courbet and Daumier, and addressed rather the fundamental question of how to best achieve 'realistic' representation of the scenery and events around them. Manet was definitely a social type, his work reflecting the everyday life of the petit-bourgeois in an uncritical manner. The younger Monet's objectivity led him away from any interest in people, turning his attention rather to the landscape and cityscape. For all their contrast in subject matter, these two paintings are united in their straightforward representation of aspects of Parisian life in the 1860s, and by their various attempts to come to terms with new ways of representing movement, light and solid form. Manet's selective focus, clearly revealed in his preparatory sketch, is an acknowledgement of the way in which the human eye would 'read' such a crowd scene in reality.

CLAUDE MONET
GARE ST LAZARE, 1877
Musée D'Orsay, Paris

cultural and intellectual centre, a bastion of emerging European civilization. By the fourteenth century the city was adorned with the great medieval churches of Saint-Germain-des-Près, Notre Dame and Saint-Chapelle, and the first royal palace at the Louvre had been built; within the new walls, streets had been paved and the capital established as the seat of *Parlement* and of the States-General, the two major governing bodies of France. Medieval representations of the city – usually crude plans – tend to concentrate naturally upon its importance as an ecclesiastical, scholarly and administrative centre.

During the Hundred Years' War the city fell into English hands but was retrieved in 1436, only to be ravaged by the Black Death a few years later. It would be another 400 years before the city was invaded again, but disruption often came from within. The wealthy merchants and tradesmen of Paris constituted a formidable political entity with which any successful monarch had to tread carefully. They had pressed for, and got, their own municipal government; in 1358 a commune had been declared, in revolt against the Dauphin Charles V. This problem would not go away. The Fronde riots of

CAMILLE PISSARRO
THE LOUVRE ON A SNOWY MORNING, 1902
National Gallery, London

1648–53 against the monarchy were centred on Paris and the Ile de France; in 1789 food riots in the capital started the trouble, in 1830 and 1848 the urban proletariat rose up again, and in 1871 another short-lived commune was declared, being brought to an end with the declaration of the Third Republic. The problems over the years were often as much to do with urban overcrowding as with objections to royal authority.

The Valois dynasty (1328–1594) maintained Paris as their capital, although the focal centre of the court and the attendant arts shifted outside the city to the new palace at Fontainebleau during the sixteenth century. The Renaissance within the city was marked by the erection of the Italianate churches of St Eustache (1532–89) and St Etienne-du-Mont (1545). The Wars of Religion following the Reformation caused a huge rift in French society and brought about the downfall of the Valois kings and, in the figure of Henry IV, the establishment of the Bourbon dynasty.

Paris emerged from the Reformation as a renewed symbol of Catholic preeminence in northern Europe (a role confirmed by the bloody excesses of the St Bartholomew's Day massacres of Protestant Huguenots in 1572). Under Marie de'Medicis, Cardinal Richelieu and Louis XIII Paris was to become the artistic and intellectual capital of Europe, and the embellishment of the city as a Catholic Baroque centre to rival Rome began. The high priest of Roman Baroque architecture, Gianlorenzo Bernini, was invited to design a new section of the Louvre (his plans were not accepted, but substantial rebuilding started in 1624); a residence for Marie de'Medicis, the Luxembourg Palace, was begun in 1615. The great Baroque domes of the Sorbonne church (1635), Val-de-Grace (1645–65) and Les Invalides (1679) were built in direct competition with the basilicas of the Holy City.

By 1650 the walls enclosed about 1400 acres (567 hectares), which was not large by contemporary standards. Louis XIV (in power 1643–1715), secure behind his national *barrière de fer*, demolished many of the fortifications and opened out the centre of the city by creating the Place Vendôme and the Place des Victoires and having the Tuileries gardens redesigned on a grand scale. However, the Fronde revolts in the city decided him to move the court, and much of the administrative machinery of government, to a splendid new palace at Versailles (see South of Paris chapter). The emergence of a new attitude to nature and the landscape which coincided with the Counter-Reformation and found majestic expression at Versailles has already been discussed. Although during Louis' long reign many acres of canvas included treatments of the landscape, these were usually celebrations of Louis' victorious absolutism, man dominating both the battlefield and nature in his formal gardens at Versailles.

With the regency of Philippe, Duke of Orléans, after Louis XIV's death, the court and high society returned to Paris. We gain an idea of their lifestyle from the paintings of Watteau, Fragonard and Boucher – a world of carefree flirtation, game-playing, nostalgia and sly eroticism. The economy had been bankrupted by Louis XIV's wars and economic policies, and the aristocracy withdrew into a life of fantasy in their apartments and gardens. The paintings of exterior views left to us are similarly fantastic – nature is an extension of the boudoir, as resplendent and sensous as silk bed-sheets. However, an associate of Fragonard's, Hubert Robert (1733–1808), retained a sensitivity to everyday affairs, and his paintings of the street scenes and views of Paris immediately prior to the Revolution provide a valuable insight into the reality of urban life at the time. He was hardly a realist – he trained classically, and his career was founded on elaborate decorative cycles for great houses; he later became Keeper of Pictures for Louis XIV, and was one of the first Curators of the Louvre. Nevertheless, like many figures during the Enlightment his intellectual interests were various and his nature inquisitive. Like Hogarth in England, he had an acute eye for the detail and curiosities of everyday life and recorded these avidly. But where Hogarth was, by the end of his career, exhibiting alongside the classical landscapes of Wilson and the Romantic landscape masterpieces of Gainsborough, not to mention a formidable body of topographic artists, across the Channel in France a resurgence of interest in classical art and a consequent attachment to the Italian landscape precluded any development of Robert's rather limited genre.

Thus it is that in Paris, as elsewhere in France, we do not see the emergence of a true native topographic or view-painting tradition until the beginning of the nineteenth century. The great events of the 1789 Revolution had been widely recorded, in paintings and prints, and these may have served to instill in the French a fresh sensitivity to their surroundings. The Bastille, for example, was probably represented more frequently after its destruction in 1789 than in the many years it stood. Two other factors also came into play: in the wake of the period of the Terror and the Directoire (1795–99), a new cultural invigoration – embodied in the figure of the First Consul and future emperor, Napoleon Bonaparte – became apparent. This manifested itself in Paris in the construction of a series of ambitious architectural projects. The process had begun in 1784 when a new city wall, about 24 miles (39 kilometres) long was constructed. This was not to protect the inhabitants from outsiders, but rather to protect the tax farmers, who levied a toll on all incoming traffic, from the populace. The main gates of this wall were designed in a high Neoclassical manner, fashionable in France and favoured by the young Republic, and in the years of Napoleon's empire the city began to be replanned as an imperial capital with major landmarks thrown up in similar style. The Panthéon was completed (1792), the Madeleine church (1807), the rue de Rivoli area around the Tuileries (1802) and, of course, the Arc de Triomphe (1806). Foreign visitors to the capital were impressed by the changes, and sometimes painted them, but native artists on the whole failed to follow their example.

The second feature, which may have helped to clear the air in the arts, was the substantial decline in private patronage. The greater proportion of that class which had, before the Revolution, invested heavily in the arts and had maintained a rarified dictum in taste, were now murdered or in exile.

The city emerged from this period in a confident mood, but somewhat shackled by its turbulent political

PIERRE AUGUSTE RENOIR
THE LUNCHEON OF THE BOATING PARTY, 1881
Phillips Collection, Washington DC

◀ MAURICE VLAMINCK
ON THE BANKS OF THE SEINE, undated
Collection Buhrle Schalk, Zürich

ROBERT DELAUNAY
THE EIFFEL TOWER, 1910–1911
Philadelphia Museum of Art

past – a turmoil which would not really settle until the establishment of the Third Republic in 1870. The clinging conservatism which was fostered by the conquering nations following their defeat of Bonaparte, and which was embodied in the restoration of the French throne beneath the ample posteriors of Charles X (in power 1824–30), Louis-Philippe (1830–48) and Napolean III (1848–70), also meant that reactionary institutions such as the Académie des Beaux-Arts were greatly bolstered. The classicism of the Revolutionary years was supported as the accepted style of art, but now existed alongside the Romanticism which was the legacy of Napoleon's doomed but heroic career.

The etchings of Charles Meryon (1821–68) portray the capital as a city with its roots in the past, grappling with the present. His work was almost exclusively composed of views of Paris, and in mood his pictures evoke much of the sense of impersonal threat and individual dispossession which Dickens' novels set in contemporary London captured so well. Paris was on the brink of a large-scale industrial expansion. Its population in 1820 had reached three-quarters of a million and, although the heart of the city contained great modern architectural improvements and monuments, these were punctuated by burgeoning slum areas and a morass of squalid housing dating back several centuries.

Meryon saw this schizophrenic characteristic, and exploited it. He was well equipped to do so. Born illegitimate, the son of an English doctor and a ballet dancer, he studied mathematics then entered the navy, serving in the South Seas. Towards the end of the 1840s he began painting, but due to colour-blindness turned to etching. Contemporary accounts describe a melancholic, hypersensitive man, tormented by his background and suffering a persecution mania. In 1858 he was briefly in a mental hospital, and he spent his last two years in the notorious asylum at Charenton. His major series of etched views of Paris, *Eaux-fortes sur Paris* (1850–54) reveal on the one hand a city of resplendent architectural riches in views of Notre Dame and St Etienne-du-Mont, of bridges and of picturesque streets and lanes; on the other hand the city emerges as a nightmarish labyrinth of buildings, a monstrous urban entity in which tiny ant-like figures swarm and scuttle among the monolithic architecture. This double vision embodies both aspects of the Romantic mood; nostalgic historicism, the taste for the quaint and medieval, and the lurking undefined threat which constantly haunts humanity's footsteps.

Meryon's work was admired by Romantic writers such as Victor Hugo and the critic Charles Baudelaire, whose poetry Meryon read, and of which his etchings in turn remind us in their obscure hints of life's terrors. Baudelaire was an avowed admirer and supporter of many of the Realist artists of the 1840s and 1850s, especially of the leading Parisian painter and lithographer Honoré Daumier (1808–79). Principally a figurative artist, and a prolific cartoonist in the radical press, the sheer amount of Daumier's graphic work builds up a comprehensive picture of Paris in the mid-nineteenth century. With a journalist's keen nose for current vogues and developments and a sharp eye for everyday detail, Daumier portrayed urban society at all levels from humble washerwomen to his favourite political targets, the upper middle classes of lawyers, the legislature, notaries and politicians. His radicalism can be felt in the compassion with which he portrayed the former and the vitriol he poured on the latter. Details of the cityscape in his work are minimal but telling; it is the activities he portrayed which give us an insight into the workings and life of Paris at the time – the bustle and double-dealing of the law courts; the leisured *petit-bourgeois* at the theatre; the rather dry and gloomy interiors of apartment houses, with their strict and literal social stratification – *concièrges* and services on the ground floor, the wealthy middle class on the first, lower middle class on the second, artisans on the third, and the destitute, drunk and bohemian in the draughty, dripping garrets; the urban artisans (painted in warm, richly-worked watercolours,

EDOUARD VUILLARD
PUBLIC GARDEN, 1894
Musée National d'Art Moderne, Paris

PIERRE BONNARD
DINING ROOM WITH A VIEW, 1913
Minneapolis Institute of Art

giving a sense of enduring nobility to the subjects, similar to Millet's paintings); and the dubious wonders of the modern cityscape, revealed and transformed by balloons and trams and trains.

Daumier's political leanings became most clear when he portrayed the urban insurrection of 1834 which culminated in the massacre at rue Transonian, and, almost 40 years later, the horrors of the Franco-Prussian war and the Commune. For all the froth, fashion and gaiety popularly associated with Paris, it should not be forgotten that the history of the city in the nineteenth century was in reality one of regular violent disruption and simmering urban discontent.

Edouard Manet (1832–83) also found it impossible to ignore these violent upheavals. During the period of the Prussian siege of Paris and the Commune (1870–71) he produced a large number of lithographs of the atrocious scenes of humiliation, devastation and death in the streets. By this time he was established in the vanguard of contemporary art. Almost ten years earlier he had begun to portray Paris and Parisian society in a manner which combined a cool perception of the unruffled surface of this modern urban world with a sense of knowing irony. His *Déjeuner sur l'Herbe* 1863 (see Introduction) looked back not only to Renaissance and classical art, but also the popular and voyeuristic *fêtes champêtres* of Watteau and Fragonard which had charmed and flattered the French cultivated élite at the beginning of the eighteenth century. The suggestion that such a morally ambiguous scene could take place in, say, the contemporary Luxembourg Gardens was found to be tasteless and gratuitous, however. A similar response met his updated treatment of the classical nude in his portrait of a prostitute, *Olympia* (1863). In *Concert in the Tuileries Gardens*, painted the previous year, Manet presented an uncritical view of a typical Parisian middle-class gathering – albeit already employing his flat areas of colour, loose, out-of-focus treatment of detail and strangely selective light. It is very much the work of a 'painter of modern life' in its attention to details of fashion and in its choice of subject in general. The controversial canvases of the following year seem a natural development.

Baudelaire coined the term 'painter of modern life' in an essay praising the work of Constantin Guys (1802–92), a kind of visual journalist who delighted in recording the ephemeral life of street fashions; his work again reflected the life of the city, if concentrating mainly on the wealthier citizens of the Second Empire.

It was with the Impressionists that a sudden flood of Parisian views occurred. The reasons for this were threefold: their criteria for selecting suitable subject matter, the substantial rebuilding of Paris during the Second Empire, between 1850 and 1870, and the consequent establishment of Paris as a major industrial, economic and cultural centre.

The nature of Impressionist art determined that the artists' subject matter could only be the everyday world about them. There was a conscious rejection of tradition on the one hand and Baudelaire's naturalistic aesthetic was also influential, but fundamentally Impressionism relied on direct observation of the world, in daylight (thus largely precluding traditional studio work, still lifes, nudes and so on). Most of the Impressionist painters began their careers in Paris, working or training in various studios and *ateliers*, and first coming into contact with each other there. Although rural landscape formed a major aspect of their output, early examples of these tended to be produced on brief excursions from the city (see North of Paris and Normandy chapters). Many of the group latterly lived outside Paris (mainly prompted by the Franco-Prussian war of 1870–71), but some of them were by nature and instinct urban animals; Manet, Renoir and Degas remained fairly rooted in Paris, and found their subjects there. It was in the capital that the vital influences and ingredients which contributed to the formation of Impressionism first came together.

During the 1850s and 1860s Paris itself had undergone a major transformation which inevitably drew attention to the fabric of the city and the ways of life pursued within it. Between 1841 and 1845 the city had been extended by the construction of a huge fortified wall about 30 miles (48 kilometres) in circumference (which today, with the addition of the Bois de Boulogne, defines the central administrative district of Paris, and immediately within which runs the notorious *Periphérique*). It was erected by the timid Second Republic, fearful of a renewal of the armed foreign intervention which marked the fall of Napoleon. Concentrically, about a mile within this, lay the legal limits of the city as determined by the wall of 1784. Within the latter, by 1850, the density of population was enormous (between 1817 and 1861 the population grew from 714,000 to 1,696,000); courtyards, gardens and small parks had been overbuilt, houses were extended upwards, and in some areas, especially in the east of the city, streets were reduced to little more than tracks. The only municipal parks were the Champs Elysées and the Place des Vosges; in addition there were the nationally-owned parks of the Luxembourg Gardens, the Jardin des Plantes and the Tuileries.

This crowded city bred disease and social discontent which boiled over in street fighting and class warfare in 1848. Both the burgeoning squalor and the problem of civic riot control prompted the newly elected President, Louis Napoleon (later Emperor Napoleon III), to inaugurate a massive programme of demolition, replanning and rebuilding. The Prefect of the Seine, Baron Haussmann, gouged out many of the slums, thrust broad new boulevards across whole districts and reordered in a grand manner the ancient central district around the Palais-Royal, the Louvre and the Tuileries. Areas of development and building moved out beyond the 1784 walls to fill the space formed by the 1845 fortifications, and here were sited the great regional railway termini. The docks along the Seine were replanned, and a great modern public market was built on the site of old Les Halles. The Paris Opéra was completed. The parks of Buttes-Chaumont, Monceau and Montsouris were laid out, the Bois de Boulogne was landscaped as a massive pleasure ground outside the fortifications at the western

LOUIS VIVIN
THE CATHEDRAL OF NOTRE DAME, 1933
Musée d'Art Moderne de la Ville de Paris

end of the city and the similarly proportioned Bois de Vincennes was established to the east. It was an exercise in public works on an unparalleled scale, and allowed Napoleon almost to realize his dream: 'I want to be a second Augustus,' he had written in 1842, 'because Augustus . . . made Rome a city of marble.'

The overall effect of this programme was to thrust Paris forward as the exemplary modern city of Europe, an achievement crowned by the siting of the *Expositions Universelles* there in 1867 and in 1880. The Eiffel Tower was built, in centennial celebration of the Revolution, for the latter *Exposition*. Both events were a great fillip to tourism, and with the emphasis placed upon the arts at the *Expositions* Paris rapidly reaffirmed her role as the centre of Western art. Among Americans Paris acquired a cult status which can be traced from the novels of Henry James to those of Henry Miller. The first American artists to work in Paris, presaging a deluge in the early years of the twentieth century, included Whistler and the talented Impressionist Mary Cassatt.

The young Impressionists were caught up in the excitement and beauty of the birth of modern Paris. Monet's paintings of the Gare St Lazare (apart from satisfying his interest in atmospheric effects) are hymns to modern technology. Older edifices were viewed in a new light. The changing face of the city matched their interest in the changing light and seasons. Pissarro especially studied the city under various guises – fog, snow, at daybreak and dusk, often drawing dramatic fresh treatments and moods from the same scene. Renoir captured the mood of the people, an optimistic, buoyant and fairly wealthy urban populace thronging the refreshed *places* and new broad boulevards, while Degas, when drawn away from the perfumed delicacies of the ballet, mixed with the crowds at Longchamps racecourse. The atmosphere could not be more different from the gloom of Meryon and Daumier a mere 20 years beforehand.

The Impressionists did much to liberate art from the studio-bound atmosphere favoured by the Académie des Beaux-Arts; they introduced a new freedom to the palette and they also gave Paris a modern look. Much of this arose from their interest in eye-catching design and visual immediacy. In the former they were much influenced by Japanese prints, taking from them the oblique design and the unusual viewpoint, a technique more suited to the experience of the rush and clamour of street life than to rural landscapes. Their desire to capture a sense of immediacy was influenced by photography, its ability to arrest motion and the often accidental compositional impact of a snapshot.

ALBERT MARQUET
QUAI CONTI UNDER SNOW, c.1906
Coll. Marquet, Paris

Many of the various strands which came together in Impressionism were later unravelled and pursued as individual avenues of artistic endeavour by the so-called Post-Impressionists. This name is really no more than a useful collective term for a wide variety of artists whose careers occurred after the main Impressionist period (c. 1865–85), and who, in various ways, profited by the experience of Impressionism. The heightened colour of the Impressionists was turned into a symbolic vehicle by the Pont-Aven school and the Nabis (see Brittany chapter); their re-evaluation of methods of applying paint in analytical brush strokes was taken on the one hand to a quasi-scientific extreme by Seurat (see Rivers chapter), and on the other as a means of modelling solid objects by Cézanne (see Provence chapter). Van Gogh and Soutine would see in their bright colours, dynamic compositions and patterned brushwork a new means of deeply personal spiritual and psychological expression (see Mountains and Provence chapters). Finally, the Impressionist obsession with light would bear strange fruit in the early experiments of the Fauve painters and Matisse (see Mediterranean chapter). Nearly all of the Post-Impressionists began their careers in Paris, mastering the Impressionist manner, and indeed the later work of Monet and Pissarro is so far removed from their original work in the 1860s and 1870s as to be termed Post-Impressionist (see North of Paris and Normandy chapters).

If Monet took the Gare St Lazare as a symbol of modernism, a handful of years later the Eiffel Tower readily provided a similar motif for Seurat (1889) and Robert Delaunay (1910). The tower was originally painted in bright enamel colours and, with its simple, graceful form, it was a bespoke subject for Seurat's experiments with geometric form and Divisionist colour. The same qualities appealed to Delaunay, although his interests were closely involved in the development of the abstract geometric interplay of colours. Although cool and seemingly removed from his subject, Seurat remained a figurative painter.

The Nabis were a group of painters who were influenced by the Pont-Aven group's interest in the abstract symbolic virtues of colour and by the general Impressionist interest in Japanese art. Among the Nabis, Edouard Vuillard (1868–1940) and Pierre Bonnard (1867–1947) developed in the years around the turn of the century a heightened form of Impressionism which exploited the decorative and evocative qualities of extremely bright colours. Many of their subjects were quietly domestic (boudoirs and dinner tables) or gently erotic (nudes bathing or undressing) which earned them the sobriquet *Intimiste*. Their work remains primarily decorative, but the paintings they produced present a tranquil and understated view of everyday life off the boulevards in a sunny Paris.

The reputation of Paris as the capital of both France and of Western art was enhanced and confirmed in the opening decades of the twentieth century. It became a centre of pilgrimage for artists and their camp-followers from all over Europe and the United States and many of the major movements of modern times, although often the product of artists of various nationalities, found a focal point in Paris. It was here that Cubism was developed by Picasso (a Spaniard) and Braque (a Belgian). Among the Fauves, Derain and Vlaminck worked here before moving to the Mediterranean coast. The German artists of the Dada group found refuge in Paris in the 1920s and 1930s, as did many leading Russian abstract artists. Surrealism, a truly international movement, could also claim Paris as its most formative location. Those artists whose work could not easily be categorized have come to be known by another convenient but meaningless title – the School of Paris.

A major preoccupation of many early twentieth-century movements was the work of primitive and naïve artists. Collecting African and Oceanic carvings and other works of art became popular (at the same time as the science of anthropology began to develop), while paintings produced by children or naïve artists were valued as instinctive views of the world, uncluttered by artistic, aesthetic, traditional or intellectual preconceptions (this was also the time when psychoanalysis came into being). In Paris a number of 'Innocent' artists were encouraged – outstanding among them being 'Le Douanier' Rousseau, and the Post Office employee Louis Vivin (1861–1936). The former painted few pure landscapes and, although he insisted that he painted from nature, his unusual world view always remained removed from the observation of natural reality. Vivin, however, produced a great many views of Paris in a unique manner which displayed great linear and colouristic assurance and originality. His works are fresh, immensely detailed and highly personal, when viewed in total presenting an image of the capital as a cosily familiar home while revealing (like Meryon's) a sense of the city's lurking inner personality. It is tempting to suggest that, in view of his everyday employment, he was influenced by popular postcard views of the city; his selection of subjects and compositions were certainly very similar to those of the period.

Maurice Utrillo (1883–1955) also fits into this group of 'Innocent' artists, but both his style and his background reveal a greater sophistication. His mother, Susan Valadon, was a talented painter, and she encouraged him to paint as a therapeutic activity, for early in life Utrillo became an alcoholic and a drug-user, constantly in trouble with the authorities. His private life was the archetype of the Parisian bohemian '*peintre maudit*'. He almost certainly worked from postcards, and his subject matter was usually the churches and streets of his native Montmartre. From about 1910 he employed sharp perspectives and a limited palette of greys and greens which conveyed the emotional isolation and loneliness to which life can easily be reduced in a large city.

A large city is what Paris has now become. In 1964 the administrative districts of the metropolis were reorganized and more large-scale public works were inaugurated. Montmartre and the Left Bank are no longer as resonant of their bohemian associations as they were. Immigration from France's overseas colonies has altered the social fabric and balance. Five new towns have been created in the orbit of the capital, erasing many of the localities so familiar to the nineteenth-century Parisian *paysagistes*. The Paris region now occupies 2.2 per cent of the French landmass, and within this area live over 20 per cent of the population of France.

The style of the Innocents and Utrillo has been ossified by pavement artists and 'Sunday' painters, of which Paris must have more per acre than any other part of the world – for Paris has continued to retain its position in the popular consciousness as a Mecca of the arts. However, since the 1940s this reputation has in reality been difficult to support. Internationalism, the mass media and the rise of the United States have made the arts accessible to all, regardless of location. It is interesting but not surprising that the most notorious visitor to Paris in this century, that self-styled connoisseur of the arts, Adolf Hitler, was, on his single visit to the conquered capital, only interested in viewing the Opéra and the Eiffel Tower. Fortunately Paris remained an open city during the final phase of the war and escaped serious damage, although in the last two decades much modernization has substantially altered the city, not always for the better; the Beauborg (Pompidou) Centre still excites heated exchanges. Paris though was never a sacred cow on the scale of, say, Rome, and we are fortunate in inheriting such a rich artistic record of its changing face over the last century and a half. Tourism, of course, has altered too. The whistle-stop tours of European capitals are less popular than they were, and the modern traveller is often keen to see as much as possible of the countryside. Here too there is a rich artistic legacy, not just in the immediate environs of the capital but much further afield.

MAURICE UTRILLO
THE CHURCH OF SACRE COEUR DE MONTMARTRE AND THE CHÂTEAU DES BROUILLARDS, c.1912
Museu de Arte de São Paulo

SOUTH OF PARIS

The area to the immediate south of Paris remains one of the richest reservoirs of recent historical landscape in France. From the foothills of the formerly powerful dukedoms of Burgundy and Champagne, the most famous wine-growing regions in the world, a broad vale extends in a huge arc around the southern edge of Paris through which flow the rivers Aube and Loing (tributaries of the Seine) and the Loire. Heavily wooded, much of this vale remains a kind of 'green belt' around the conurbation, encompassing the medieval hunting reserve of the Forest of Fontainebleau with its areas of heathland and numerous scattered villages which for long retained a distinctly old-fashioned peasant agricultural atmosphere, despite their close proximity to Paris. In the east of the Forest lies the village of Barbizon. For many nineteenth-century day-trippers from the capital, the low rises and broad open valleys around Barbizon, dotted with other church-spired villages such as Chailly and Maincy and supporting a simple agricultural economy, provided a taste of the countryside which developed into a kind of rustic cult not dissimilar in essence to that of Hardy's Wessex in England.

Further west, the remaining Forest becomes denser around Rambouillet before opening out to the south into the rich agricultural valley of the Loire, with its many medieval and Renaissance châteaux, and to the north on to a broad cultivated plain at the heart of which rise the spired towers of Chartres cathedral.

For travellers from Paris, the region fell into two historical sections. To the south-east lay the major routes to Chalons and the trans-Alpine routes to Italy and to Lyons (the financial centre of France in the high Middle Ages and early modern period) at the head of the Rhône valley, the major commercial corridor to the Mediterranean. The importance of this route was reflected in the development along this corridor of a series of major medieval trade fairs.

South-west from Paris the Loire valley, with its powerful seigneurial seats – Blois, Amboise, Chambord, Chenonceaux, Chinon and Azay-le-Rideau – was a political centre and the heart of Gallic France which needed to be closely bound to the capital. Routes to Orléans on the Loire were strengthened and a series of new towns (or villages, *villeneuves*) established as a means of consolidating political control and influence. The region south of Paris was therefore always of considerable interest and importance to both the monarchy and the population of the capital in general.

Fontainebleau was long a royal residence away from the noise and vapours of Paris, its chief attraction being the excellent hunting in the vast forest. Louis IV resided there, Philip IV and Louis XIII were born there, and

HUBERT ROBERT
THE GARDENS AT VERSAILLES, 1774–75
Musée de Versailles

THEODORE ROUSSEAU
THE COUNTRYSIDE
Museo Civico, Barletta

Theodore Rousseau remains the most outstanding painter of the Barbizon School, and was the first of that group to live and work in the Barbizon region of the Forest of Fontainebleau. The district offered a variety of landscapes – few of them actually heavily wooded, the region tending rather towards open scrubland with scattered groups of trees and long open vistas. The area supported mixed peasant agriculture, on the sparser hilltops sheep and cattle would be grazed, and around the scattered villages land, where possible, was put under the plough. Rousseau's work encompasses all these variations (his output was fairly large); he rarely needed to add anything to a simple landscape view to gain his effects, for the rich tonality of his earth colours (now often rather distorted due to ageing and poor varnishes) and the immense solidity of his forms built up a simple but resonant statement. His perception of light, although not innovatory, was certainly dramatic, playing off sparkling highlights and bright skies against cool, plunging shadows. Rousseau's lack of sentimentality and reasonably objective view have left us an immutable record of the mid-nineteenth century French rural landscape.

Francis I rebuilt the residence from c.1530 as the centrepiece of the French Renaissance (see Introduction), the project being expanded and elaborated by Henry IV. Among the many artists who worked at Fontainebleau, the few landscapists were notable for importing and developing the classical landscape manner. The dark, deciduous environs of the palace were not considered worthy subjects for painting at the time.

Just over a century later, in 1661, Louis XIV began the realization of his ambitious plans for a major new palace complex some 40 miles (64 kilometres) to the north-west, and much nearer the capital, at Versailles. Again originally a hunting lodge, built by Louis XIII, the *raison d'être* of the new palace was far removed from the hunting and Renaissance humanism of Fontainebleau. Here the arts and nature were harnessed in the service of the state to produce an enormous work of regal propaganda, the official seat of the Sun King, the centre of the largest absolutist court in Europe, and an overpowering and awe-inspiring statement of the ascendancy of the French monarchy. The palace was painted many times, but most often as a backdrop to high Baroque portraits of Louis XIV in martial postures. After Louis' death the palace became as much a burden to the

THEODORE ROUSSEAU
LANDSCAPE STUDY IN THE FOREST OF FONTAINEBLEAU
Louvre, Paris

NARCISSE DIAZ DE LA PEÑA
GYPSIES GOING TO A FAIR,
1844
Museum of Fine Arts, Boston

taxpayers as many of the Sun King's other grandiose gestures. The logistics of maintaining such an enormous residence were formidable. Among the first naturalistic views of the palace were a number of paintings concentrating on the day-to-day life of Versailles, painted by Hubert Robert. These were a natural development from his occasional interest in *genre* street scenes and views in Paris (see Paris chapter).

At the time that Robert painted at Versailles Louis XV modified both the interior and the gardens, and staged a number of lavish *fêtes* in and around the palace. The complex itself and the relocation of much of the administrative bureaucracy in the formerly tiny village naturally stimulated the local economy enormously, but it comes as no surprise that some of the opening scenes of the Revolution of 1789 were played out there.

By the beginning of the nineteenth century, in France as elsewhere in Europe, city life was beginning to be recognized as something less than salubrious. Paris was probably no more unhealthy than any European city of comparable size at the time – indeed industrialization there was slow to develop, although overcrowding was becoming an increasing problem. The proximity of a forested region to the south of the capital encouraged an increasingly mobile urban populace to forsake the city for brief excursions. Fontainebleau itself became a popular spring and autumn resort, and with the (late) development of a French sensitivity to nature and natural surroundings, there emerged the first French school of native landscape painting based around the village of Barbizon, some 10 miles (16 kilometres) north-west of Fontainebleau. Here, in the late 1830s and the 1840s, assembled a group of painters who might broadly be termed Romantic, and whose influence bridged an important span between the Romanticism of the early years of the nineteenth century and the Realism which prefigured Impressionism.

The central figure and leader of the Barbizon group was Théodore Rousseau (1812–67). He studied under the classical painter Lethière, and his early work shows a confident grasp of classical structure and pathos. These elements remained an essential ingredient in his painting for the rest of his career, and his subject matter, forest pools, deserted plains, the edges of woods or – his favourite motif – single, spectacular trees, always retained a classical feeling of generalization and of heroic grandeur, albeit in a Romantic, pantheistic manner. What set Rousseau and his followers apart from the classical tradition was the influence they absorbed from contemporary English landscape painters (Constable and Bonington) and, more especially, from the Dutch school of the seventeenth century (notably Ruisdael and Hobbema). In the latter, the Barbizon painters discovered a manner at once removed from the nostalgic Mediterranean scenery of true classical landscape painting to something distinctly closer to home and more familiar and brought to the canvas with all the compositional mechanism and fluency of Baroque painting.

The importance of composition in his work was admitted by Rousseau: 'By composition I understand that which is within us, entering as far as possible into the external reality of things.' This quotation also underlines the aspect of the Barbizon group's work which links them more closely with their Dutch and classical forebears than with the Impressionists of the following generation: they were interested primarily in the external appearance of things. Light, colour and visual perception were never considered problems or worthy of further analysis. Strangely, despite Rousseau's avowed emphasis on composition and his interest in Japanese woodcuts (so influential on artists later in the century), his work seems in total rather programmatic and compositionally unadventurous.

From 1836 Rousseau's 'external reality' was the landscape around Barbizon. Corot and Bertin had worked in the region before, but the sheer amount of paintings and sketches Rousseau produced in the area – he became known as the Hermit of Barbizon – claim it as his own. One would expect this concentration on one region to produce a strong feeling for the locality similar to that achieved by the Pont-Aven school in Brittany or by Cezanne and Van Gogh in Provence, but this somehow eluded Rousseau. This is partly due to his intense and direct concentration on the careful observation and representation of the smaller details of the landscape – the tectonic structure of a range of hills, the architecture of a tree, the dense massing of forms in a wood; yet at the same time this attention to detail remained subordinate to the unification of all the elements into the final composition.

Rousseau was definitely the most inspired pure landscapist of the group. Other members played out a variety of lesser variations on his central theme. Narcisse Diaz (c. 1807–76) often peopled his landscapes with gypsy women, Jules Dupré (1811–89), a close friend of Rousseau, toned down the natural vitality of his colleague's style to produce a gentler, more elegiac effect.

Two older artists provided valuable personal links with other traditions. Paul Huet (1803–69) had travelled widely and had been in touch with both Constable and Bonington. His technique was very much derived from the English tradition of Romantic view painting, producing many vivid and expressive sketches of scenery glimpsed on travels which would then be worked up into more formal canvases in the studio. It should be noted that none of the Barbizon group, except the peripheral Daubigny (see Rivers chapter), insisted on painting *en plein air*. Georges Michel (1763–1843) was employed in restoring the Dutch collection in the Louvre, which provided a valuable insight into that tradition for the Barbizon painters. His own work concentrated on particularly unpicturesque subjects – muddy lanes and heaths – but he remains the great master of the French Romantic sky. The careful articulation of tones needed to bring to life the prevalent shower-filled clouds of northern Europe led him to be considered one of the more sophisticated landscape colourists of the early nineteenth century.

Colour, or rather their lack of it, held most of the Barbizon group back. Their palettes were restricted to the greys and greens most apparent in the scenery they saw before them. Unlike Corot, they failed to grasp the modelling qualities inherent in colour when modified by light. Only Daubigny, on the outskirts of the Barbizon group, understood the importance of light as a medium of transition between the object and its realization in paint. Thus the Barbizon group never came close to the re-evaluation of the methods of perceiving a landscape which was the triumph of the Impressionists. Barbizon naturalism was quite literal. (It is interesting to note that the Impressionists rarely used green – they regarded it as an unnatural composite colour, and sought to create the effect of green by using juxtapositions, but not mixtures, of blues and yellows.)

One other outstanding member of the Barbizon group, Jean-François Millet (1814–75), worked in a manner stylistically removed from the pure landscapists. Their pictures rarely included people. For Millet, the people of the land were of central importance. He was born in a small farming village in Normandy, and only left this peasant background to become a painter in 1834. He studied under the battle-painter Charles Langlois in Cherbourg, then went to Paris to work under Paul Delaroche and at the *Atèlier Suisse*. His early work comprises portraits and pastoral subjects in an erotic vein, similar in many ways to the decorative fantasies popular at the beginning of the eighteenth century. It was not until 1849 that he moved from the capital to Barbizon, where his preoccupations suddenly centred on the landscape and its people. There he rapidly developed a unique style of epic naturalism.

The landscapes he painted in his first ten years at Barbizon remained secondary to the large foreground figures of peasants, presented in a noble, slightly sentimental manner which we recognize today as an aspect of 'Realism'. Details of the landscape are subdued in order to emphasize the figures; the characteristic view is of the flat plain around Chailly, with distant village and

GEORGES MICHEL
THE STORM, c.1820–30
Art Institute, Chicago

Georges Michel's close contact with the work of Dutch seventeenth-century masters (he restored pictures at the Louvre) led him to emulate something of their style. However, unlike them, he worked *en plein air*, and ranks as one of the first French artists to do so. His work is dramatic in its tonality and heightened lighting effects, although strangely Michel remained obscure and largely unrecognized all his life. Like his close English contemporary, Constable, he was content to work in a limited area – painting for the most part the fields and heaths immediately around Paris. Indeed, he contended that an area of four square miles would provide him with sufficient material for a lifetime of painting. This work appeals to the modern eye particularly because of its very loose technique. It is not, in fact, a finished painting, but rather an *ébauche*, that is an oil sketch in which the principal colour elements, lighting scheme and physical elements are roughly blocked out. Many of the French Romantics expressed a preference for the rough, expressive finish of the *ébauche* in comparison to the high standards of finish required by the Academic Salons. It would not be long, however, before this type of sketch would be regarded more widely as being an acceptable finished work.

church steeple on the horizon – a scheme which served to project the monumental foreground figures forward. These popular paintings – such as *The Winnower* (1848), *The Sower* (1850), *The Gleaners* (1857) and *The Angelus* (1855–57) – are stripped bare of the sort of sophistication associated with Romantic painting, or even that of his fellow 'Realists', Daumier and Courbet. They represent a combination of Millet's own understanding of peasant life, an urge to create monumentality (a traditional trait in both Classical and Romantic painting) and the sort of sentimentality with which he had been toying in his early works.

There is no evidence in Millet's work of this period of any interest in natural colour or in light such as we might expect – both elements are subordinate to his theme, as is the treatment of the landscape. Indeed, the style of painting itself is not distinguished – Millet's drawings and woodcuts are on the whole more successful. However, within their own terms the paintings remain undeniably great, and fulfil all the artist's aspirations.

In later life Millet turned more towards pure landscape and occasionally travelled beyond Barbizon, returning to his native Normandy and visiting the Auvergne (see Mountains chapter). In his drawings and pastels of the

JEAN-FRANÇOIS MILLET
THE ANGELUS, 1855–57
Louvre, Paris

JEAN-FRANÇOIS MILLET
SPRING, 1868–73
Louvre, Paris

Millet's mature works move beyond the normal limits of Realism, and begin to introduce a spiritual or religious element, giving them a stature and resonance unsurpassed in Realist art. The effect is produced with superficial ease in figure paintings, where the reduction of form and detail to a bare minimum emphasizes our involvement with the characters. This particular painting (left) had a special meaning for Millet, as his peasant grandmother had always stopped to pray for the dead when the Angelus was rung. To achieve a similar effect in pure landscape (above) required considerable application. The details of the scene are more carefully realized, the palette much lighter and more delicate, and the daring interplay of patchy light and the soaring rainbow build up an extraordinary epic of Nature as a creative, living force.

1860s and 1870s a more direct, but still unsophisticated, appreciation of the natural landscape is revealed. Nevertheless, the worked-up oil paintings such as the peculiar *Starry Night* (1855) or *Spring* (1868–73) are still imbued with a strong, semi-mystical and symbolic quality not far removed from his epic peasant canvases. Millet remained in truth a loner, hardly a man of visionary qualities but a painter with undeniable vision, whose work is associated with the Barbizon group more by geographical coincidence than by stylistic or ideological similarity.

The young Impressionists Pissarro, Monet, Sisley and Renoir began their careers in Paris (see Paris chapter) and in the early 1860s followed their *plein air* inclinations by taking painting trips to Barbizon. However, they soon discovered the more urbane pleasures of the lower Seine valley (see North of Paris chapter). They were undoubtedly originally attracted to Barbizon by its reputation as a centre for *paysagistes*. However, one of the leading lights of nineteenth-century French landscape painting, and one of the Impressionists' enduring heroes, lived in his later years not at Barbizon but at Ville d'Avray, on the outskirts of south-west Paris, midway between St Cloud and Versailles.

Jean Baptiste Camille Corot (1796–1875) made of this small village a recurring motif as intimately his own as Monet's water-garden or Cézanne's Mt Ste Victoire. He painted the village from many different angles, in different moods and in different styles, drawing on his by then immense repertoire of technique (his early paintings and mature style are examined in the Rivers chapter). By 1850 his gradual dissolution of the elements of the landscape into a poetic unity had begun. He developed this style increasingly over the next 20 years, to the extent that he was even accused of formlessness. It was an approach which acknowledged more clearly than that of any of his contemporaries the paramount importance of light as not only an apprehendable feature of the natural world, but as an agent which made the natural world visible and whole. He reached this position instinctively, and his method was wholly painterly; it had nothing in common with the analytical and colouristic disciplines of the Impressionists, but strangely it had more in common with many of their later works – the dissolving colour harmonies of Monet after 1890 or the decorative Divisionism of Pissarro in the 1880s.

Corot's later landscapes around Ville d'Avray often seemed to take the observation of nature only as a starting point, upon which his elaborate style built up a fantastic vision of Arcadian nature. The paintings are fundamentally tonal essays in delicate greys and greens, suffused with a silvery light which seems altogether artificial. When compared to his figure studies of the same period, the constructional importance of his handling of light becomes clearer – the figures are immensely solid and yet modelled purely in terms of tones arising from the fall of light, reminiscent of Rembrandt and prefiguring the ambiguous solidity achieved by Cézanne. It is not surprising that Monet would later remark: 'Corot was everything!'

Corot's long career predated and prefigured the Barbizon painters, and at the end it overshadowed them. The Forest of Fontainebleau long remained a popular site for aspiring landscapists, especially among Academic artists, and Rousseau (despite his consistent rejections by the Academy early in his career) was held in reverence by orthodox painters aghast at the temerity of the Impressionists. There is a certain irony, therefore, that numbered among the last notable painters of the Forest region we should find Cézanne. Upon his occasional trips to Paris from his refuge in Provence (see Provence chapter) he produced a number of sketches in watercolour and oil in the darker corners of the Forest. These works are far from topographic; they are rarely specifically located and concentrate on details of trees and rock formations in Cézanne's characteristic blue and green washes, crosscut and counterpoised by delicate, edgy brushwork. They demonstrate, however, when seen beside the work of the Barbizon group, the very different effects and perceptions which are offered to artists by a similar tract of land.

Today the region has lost some of its charm; the outward spread of Paris and the consequent growth of roads and motorways has carved much of it up. However, much of the Forest of Fontainebleau remains intact, the palaces of Versailles and Fontainebleau have been preserved to be enjoyed, and the Loire valley is still one of the great attractions of the French countryside. We might be hard pressed to find any of Millet's peasants tilling the land, but in the work of the Barbizon school we can recognize the ability to appreciate an essential glory in nature which remains a continuing aspect of European civilization.

JEAN BAPTISTE COROT
VILLE D'AVRAY, c.1855
National Gallery of Scotland, Edinburgh

NORTH OF PARIS

To the north of the French capital lie tracts of territory the fortunes of which have, through history, alternated between prosperity and devastation. Agriculture and trade with the Low Countries were, throughout the Middle Ages and early modern period, the mainstays of the region's wealth. Furthermore, the natural resources of coal and iron ore in the Lorraine were among the first in Europe to be heavily exploited.

However, it remained the part of France most commonly subject to invasion; it formed the garrisoned northern frontier of the Roman empire for two centuries, and subsequently was one of the first areas of the empire to fall prey to both invasion and settlement by the Germanic armies who gradually swept Roman power from western Europe after the mid-fifth century AD. Many of the English campaigners of the Hundred Years' War ravaged this countryside; the fearful bloodletting of the Thirty Years' War spilled over the Rhine from the cauldron of destruction in western Germany; Louis XIV devoted much energy to extending the northern frontiers of France into the Spanish Netherlands (Belgium) and Lorraine, at enormous cost, towards the end of the seventeenth century; and many of the key battles of the War of the Spanish Succession were played out along these new borders. The Prussian invasion of France in 1870, when Bismarck's armies swept through Metz, Verdun and Sedan before besieging Paris itself, was unfortunately only a prelude to the protracted apocalypse hammered out along the Western Front between 1914 and 1918. The price of holding the German advance along this line is still etched on the landscape. The damage wrought in the Great War enforced the rebuilding not only of the economy and the settlements of northern France but also of the landscape itself. For many Frenchmen the construction of the 'indestructible' Maginot Line and the cession of Alsace-Lorraine and the rich Saar coalfields were symbols of a new beginning. When Hitler's Panzer divisions rumbled over the border in June 1940 that beginning crumbled, to be replaced by a scenario which already seemed far too familiar.

Despite this succession of sad episodes the region encompasses many delights: in the east, rugged but not inaccessible upland forested ridges mark the Rhineland, the Hunsrück and the Ardennes border areas which give way, as the border marches westwards, to gentle chalk downlands, smooth-backed hills undulating between the

CLAUDE LORRAINE
MILL ON A RIVER, c.1627
Museum of Fine Arts, Boston

river valleys of the Meuse, the Marne, the Aisne, the Sambre, the Oise and the Somme. Lorraine still retains (like many upland areas) a regional cultural distinction apart from the rest of France, despite its early industrial development during the nineteenth century. Nearer Paris the flavour of the surviving towns and villages is often bestowed by their quintessentially Gothic churches and cathedrals, the most notable being at Rheims.

The naturally picturesque qualities of northern France caught the attention of two French painters at a comparatively early date: Jacques Callot (1592–1635) and François Desportes (1661–1740). Although Callot trained in Rome (see Introduction) he spent most of his career in and around Paris and the northwest, and was eyewitness to many of the atrocities perpetrated in the name of religion during the Thirty Years' War. The landscape of the Rhine border, with its wooden ridges and small towns perched on spurs and hillocks, provides the detailed backdrops for his printed representations of the horrors of that war. His adventures into pure landscape were limited to sketches and small engravings of unspecified scenery. The choice of subject and composition are similar to the sort of informal classical landscape studies produced by many artists in and around Rome, yet they are imbued with a freshness and crispness alien to the classical tradition. Callot was a contemporary of Claude (Le) Lorraine who was born in Lorraine and who worked there briefly from 1625 to 1627. It may not be too fanciful to suggest that the parameters of classical landscape painting which Claude espoused (see Introduction), and the taste for dramatic landscape forms which are often apparent in his work, may have some relation to his native landscape.

Desportes has left us with a strange legacy which fits uncomfortably into the story of French landscape painting. He was primarily an immensely popular painter of animals, hunting scenes and still lifes with game in the manner of the Flemish school. The backgrounds of most of his paintings were usually landscapes, but they remained subservient to the main subject of the composition. In preparing these backdrops, however, he made a number of oil studies of the region around the North of Paris which show a unique and unpretentious approach to the subject. In design they remain fairly simple, and he showed little desire to follow the classical line of altering or adapting the landscape in order to perfect the

FRANÇOIS DESPORTES
LANDSCAPE, c.1700
Musée National du Château de Compiègne

proportion and composition. These studies were made directly from nature, at a time when *'plein air'* painting was unusual, if not completely unknown. However, they remained achievements without progeny, although his delicate treatment of light and tonality looks forward to the English topographical watercolour school of the eighteenth century and the French Romantic naturalists of the nineteenth century.

Desportes tended to identify the location of his subject; Callot did not, and in this he remains true to a characteristic of French landscape painting (in both France and Italy) which persisted right up to the Impressionists. It seems that for French artists, when a landscape was sufficiently attractive to commend itself to the painter this could be regarded as a happy accident, a fortunate though largely uncommon coincidence of elements from which the painter could construct (in a classical, Platonic manner) an idealized or generalized statement about nature. They saw little point in identifying the exact views which inspired their pictures. This was even true of the Barbizon school, and underlines a fundamental difference in approach between French landscape painters and their northern European neighbours. Among English topographical painters their often careful labelling not just of sites, but of local weather conditions and times of day, emphasized their feeling that nature – wherever it was encountered, and under whatever conditions – was capable of displaying enormous beauty and splendour.

It is useful that many of the Impressionists shared this habit and the sentiment behind it, for otherwise it would be difficult to disentangle the sheer volume of work most of them produced during their often peripatetic careers.

At the heart of Impressionism, the core of the movement, were Pissarro, Monet, Bazille and Renoir, who all met in Paris between 1859 and 1862. Over the next few years they together developed the habit of painting *en plein air*, making excursions from Paris to paint the countryside. For Pissarro, the valley of the Oise held a particular fascination. Camille Pissarro (1830–1903) was a decade older than most of the other Impressionists, and a near contemporary of Manet; he was later to be regarded as a father figure within the Impressionist group. He had been born in the French West Indies and after various travels came to Paris in 1855, being immediately impressed at the Exposition Universelle by the work of Corot, Courbet and Manet. His early years in Paris were a period of broad-ranging experiment in various styles of landscape painting. Although he produced little of distinction during this time, versatility and adaptability were to become hallmarks of his career.

In 1886 Pissarro moved to Pontoise, and during the next four years became increasingly influenced by Monet's ability to present objects and scenery purely as manifestations of light and colour. From this point onwards he was to remain the most consistent of all the Impressionists, and yet the one most capable of adjusting his style to fit his new ideas. In 1869 he moved to Louveciennes, on the Seine near Paris, but in 1870, following the Prussian invasion of France, he fled to Brittany and then to London. There he worked consis-

CARL FREDRIK HILL
SEINE LANDSCAPE, 1877
Nationalmuseum, Stockholm

One very important influence on nineteenth-century French landscape painters, which is often overlooked in the English-speaking world, is that of the German and Scandinavian Romantic landscape tradition, which had a long and respectable pedigree stretching well back into the eighteenth century. Where the Dutch painters of the seventeenth century had more or less invented the non-classical European landscape form, and English painters of the eighteenth and early nineteenth century had exploited its topographic and picturesque possibilities, the Germans and Scandinavians were the first to realize fully the Romantic, almost spiritual qualities of the natural world. Many of them visited France, and although Hill was a late example of their virtuosity, Sweden's leading mid-century landscape painter approached the French landscape with an enormous authority, imbuing it with a monumental stillness and peace only found, among French painters, in the more Italienate work of Corot.

HILL

PIERRE AUGUSTE RENOIR
LA GRENOUILLÈRE, 1869
Nationalmuseum, Stockholm

CLAUDE MONET
LA GRENOUILLÈRE, 1869
Metropolitan Museum of Art, New York

Although most of the young Impressionists worked, at one stage or another, together or with older artists such as Manet, Courbet, Boudin and Whistler, the period which Monet and Renoir spent together at La Grenouillère, on the Seine just below Paris, qualifies as one of the most important formative liaisons in modern art. For it was here, among the bustle of day-trippers, and pleasure seekers afloat, that the basic ground rules of Impressionism were established. The fragmentary brushstroke, carrying single, often unmixed gobbets of colour, the recognition of the importance of reflected and refracted light in modifying local colours, the daring use of asymmetrical compositions and apparently arbitrary cut-offs of objects – all these elements were brought together for the first time. So involved were they in this experiment that their work at Grenouillère is almost indistinguishable.

ALFRED SISLEY
FLOODS AT PORT-MARLY,
1876
Musée d'Orsay

tently, and saw paintings by Turner and Constable. The following year he returned to Louveciennes to discover that the Germans had used his house as an abattoir and his store of 300 paintings as duckboards.

Pissarro retraced his steps to Pontoise, where he was joined by Paul Cézanne, whom he had first met in Paris in 1861. Together they experimented with various methods of realizing their aims in experimental brushstrokes, colour harmonies and compositional selection.

Pissarro never rejected the pictorial attractions of deep perspectives as had Monet, and tree-lined roads and the receding banks of rivers are often used as convenient structural motifs in his work. His brushwork was always fine and delicately agitated, building up a coherent illusory surface through tiny touches of paint which lent a feeling of solidity and shimmering life to his compositions. In many ways this style prefigured Divisionism. In his choice of colour Pissarro remained fairly conservative; his paintings were normally orchestrations of related hues and tones, although often the keynote of those orchestrations could be quite striking, as in *Red Roofs*.

Figures are rarely absent from Pissarro's landscapes, and he portrayed the peasant farmers and cowgirls as integral elements within the environment, devoid of the sentimentality of Millet or the monumentality of Courbet. In this, his approach to the 'real' world remains one of the most satisfying and balanced in the French landscape tradition.

During the 1880s Pissarro became increasingly influenced by the Divisionist theories of Seurat, and his

CAMILLE PISSARRO
THE BANKS OF THE OISE, PONTOISE, 1877
Private Collection

palette became more restricted as he attempted to combine the analytical brushwork and colour values of the Divisionists with the more instinctive taste for unusual light conditions and atmospheric effects of the older Impressionists.

Pissarro's consistency was a great steadying influence on his peers and he also had a formative influence on the younger artists in the last quarter of the century, not least Paul Cézanne. His son Lucien was a talented landscapist in a similar style who also worked in the Oise region.

Cézanne's work in the 1860s had toyed with sensational realism, but appeared rather unstructured. His work with Pissarro at Pontoise from 1871 was immensely important in his development: for the first time, under Pissarro's influence, Cézanne concentrated on pure landscapes painted in the open air, and within this discipline he began forging his own peculiar style which set off a flattened pictorial depth against a spatial modulation of tones. The two painters experimented with applying paint with palette knives, with brush strokes of varying size and length, and with the notion of building up a patterned surface of brush strokes. Where Pissarro developed a style of fine impasto modelling (emulated by Cézanne in *La Maison du Perdu*, 1873), the latter went on to develop more fully the structural possibilities of broad patches of paint, which became the most notable feature of his style.

It was to Auvers-sur-Oise that Vincent van Gogh came for the last few months of his life. He had discharged himself from the asylum at St Remy, near Arles, (see Provence chapter) upon hearing that his brother Theo had married in 1889. He spent a brief time in Paris and by May 1890 was in Auvers, where he lodged with Dr Paul Gachet, a psychiatrist and patron of the arts. For the next three months he painted feverishly. There is a feeling of exorcism rather than catharsis about these late works. Although his compositions were frequently less precipitous than they had been in

VINCENT VAN GOGH
WHEATFIELD, 1890
Stedelijk Museum, Amsterdam

Provence (fewer diagonals and steep perspectives appear in his landscapes), the still lifes and portraits of this period have a pronounced psychoanalytical feeling to them. His fragmented brushstrokes now assumed a desperate life of their own, dominating the lurid colours of his palette.

It seems that in landscape painting Van Gogh found at least a degree of escape from his inner turmoil. Nevertheless this notional freedom implied independence and, after months of institutional life, independence meant isolation and loneliness. Not many people choose to commit suicide in public, but it is somehow telling that Van Gogh shot himself in the head on the side of a deserted road, a setting so easily envisaged from his paintings. Characteristically, luck was against him and he suffered a further two days before finally dying.

The landscape around Paris, especially to the north of the capital, is rarely overtly picturesque. It is undoubtedly its proximity to Paris itself which led so many painters to work there. The often wide variation in their styles and approach has nevertheless given the world an impressive composite image of the Ile de France. Of course, not all those painters who trained or began their careers in Paris originally came from the capital. Many had painted their native regions before going there, and many returned to their birthplaces in later life. Also, as the aims and requirements of artists changed, so their appetite for fresh challenges, in landscape as elsewhere, grew. As the nineteenth century progressed painters worked further afield, exploring the rich possibilities of fresh landscapes often remote from Paris.

PAUL NASH
WE ARE MAKING A NEW WORLD, 1918
Imperial War Museum, London

The landscape around Paris has not always produced paintings of balance, stillness and peaceful harmony.

For Van Gogh, travelling from Provence where he had spent two lengthy periods in asylums, the landscape around Auvers-sur-Oise provided a fresh challenge for the techniques he had developed in the South. The paintings he executed here do not display the fraught anxiety of many of his Provençale works – they seem to have escaped the burgeoning, paranoic structure of his paintings of cypress trees and moonlit roads, but in doing so a new cataclysmic vigour invested his brushwork as it slips and slides out of a coherent pictorial structure as if the paint is seeking a way off the canvas. His palette too rejects inhibitions, and seeks rather the overt shock of primaries laid against one another. They are brilliant paintings from the edge of the mind.

Paul Nash, whilst serving in the trenches of the western front, encountered insanity on a less personal, grander scale: a lunacy endorsed and promoted by politicians – a madness which left its mark on the landscape itself. The combination of the subterranean half-life of the trenches, where men lived for weeks soaked in mud and covered with lice, and the peculiar distortion of the landscape wracked by incessant shell and mortar fire produced nightmare images of the world. Strangely, Nash's paintings are not violent or bitter, they have the somnolent stillness of a dreamscape, which only adds greater ironic force to the title of the picture.

RIVERS

The French landmass is physically divided and economically united by four large river systems: the Seine in the north, rising in the hills of Burgundy and travelling westwards through the Ile de France, flowing into the Channel; to the south, flowing west into the Bay of Biscay, is the Loire, its watershed stretching from Orléanais in the north to the Massif Central in the south. Further down the Biscay coast is the mouth of the Garonne, which rises in the Pyrenees and flows northwards through Gascony and Guyenne to meet the sea below Bordeaux. Finally, the Rhône, formed by the overflow from Lake Geneva and fed by the run-off from the Jura mountains and by its confluence with the Saône at Lyons, flows due south, dividing the great uplands of the Massif Central and the Alps and emptying finally into the Mediterranean. Rivers often form political boundaries but for France, closeted by seacoasts and mountains, only the Rhine and the Saar in the northwest have ever served this purpose.

Rivers have always been closely associated with human settlement and with wealth. As a source of irrigation and drainage they enjoy a close relationship with agriculture. Bridging and fording places formed natural centres for settlement, focal points for lines of communications and gathering places for travellers; Paris, Lyons, Toulouse, Rouen, Bordeaux and Nantes all began as major river crossings. Until the last 150 years, before the advent of railways and the combustion engine, the cheapest and fastest means of transport, especially for bulk goods, was by water. Classical Roman reliefs show barges laden with wine casks plying the Rhine and the Moselle while, throughout the Middle Ages, the control and flow of riverborne commerce expanded, providing an increasing source of revenue.

During the reign of Louis XIV miles upon miles of canals were dug, notably in the region north of Paris, linking the Seine to the waterways of the Low Countries, and in numerous areas south of Paris linking the rivers of the northwest with the Saône and Rhône basin. This programme culminated in the construction of the *Canal Royale* (now the *Canal du Midi*) which follows the course of the Garonne and then links Toulouse with the Mediterranean. This enormous network meant that waterborne traffic could cross the whole of France and, more importantly, Atlantic shipping could be linked with the Mediterranean, bypassing the lengthy (and often unfriendly) sea passage around the Iberian peninsula. The completion of this project allowed France to stand in the vanguard of European commerce and industrialization until the end of the eighteenth century, which in turn helps to explain the considerable regard the French have always had for their rivers.

THE LIMBOURG BROTHERS
OCTOBER FROM "LES TRÈS RICHES HEURES", PAINTED FOR THE DUKE OF BERRY,
1413–16
Condé Museum, Chantilly

Like mountains, rivers offer landscape painters of all styles and tastes particular opportunities. Unlike those of mountains, these opportunities are not static but full of movement and vitality. As a river enters its mature stage, midway between its source and its mouth, it will normally begin to follow a particular meandering pattern. This characteristic, if viewed from up- or downstream, is a ready-made method of establishing spatial depth and recession in a landscape, and has been exploited throughout the history of landscape painting. Such meanders also permit the artist to include natural serpentine forms in his composition (the serpentine was long regarded by artists as the abstract epitome or ideal of beauty). Rivers frequently offer other picturesque properties: they flow through valleys (from sharp mountain defiles to broad open vales) of their own making. These may be wooded or on the lower, more level reaches, where the valley floor is made up of alluvial soils deposited by the river over the centuries, there may be agricultural land reaching right up to the banks. Traditional crossing points may be marked by a bridge, often of some antiquity, and usually combining ingenious engineering skills with a graceful harmony of form.

Human interference with the flow of a river can produce other interesting architectural forms, ranging from the massed monumental arches of the Roman aqueduct at Nîmes, the Pont du Gard, to the dubious aesthetic appeal of the raising bridge at Langlois which seemed to so fascinate Van Gogh (presumably because its appearance reminded him of his home country, where the landscape is punctuated by locks and sluices). During the nineteenth century, when new industrial techniques were allowing architects and engineers to construct ever greater spans by using iron bracing and cantilevers, the first great masterpieces of their art were the great iron and glass canopies of railway sheds and iron bridges. It is not surprising then that painters such as the Impressionists, concerned with the beauty of the modern world, should find a certain fascination in these buildings.

The commercial life of rivers also continued to interest artists. These arteries of commerce and communication are today often hopelessly polluted or have fallen into disrepair, their surfaces at best cluttered with pleasure craft; it is perhaps difficult to conjure up the image of the great chains of frequently gaily painted barges and lighters, some under large gaffe-rigged ochre sails, some drawn along towpaths by horses, which continually criss-crossed Europe in the days before railways and motorways came to dominate.

Running water also offered one of the greatest challenges to the painter; to capture, frozen in pigment on a canvas, the constantly shifting ripples on the surface

Daubigny

▲ CHARLES FRANÇOIS DAUBIGNY
POOL WITH HERONS, 1857
Louvre, Paris

In the decades between 1830 and 1860, when landscape painting in France developed fully into a mature tradition, several artists were experimenting with different ways of resolving the problems posed in capturing faithfully the visual experience of the landscape. Corot moved from a spontaneous interpretation of the classical landscape formula towards a style based solidly on the delicate balance of colour and shape. The Barbizon School worked through a robust, journeyman style of Romantic improvisation. Daubigny's importance during this phase was as an innovative painter of water, and of the peculiar light and atmospheric effects often associated with bodies of water. He worked for the most part around Paris – sometimes at Barbizon – a well-drained region with an even spread of gentle rivers and streams, pools lying on the loamy soil, and villages and towns clustered around confluences and bridging or fording points. He often lived and worked on his floating studio – a converted boat. Water, it seems, provided an essential medium for him linking the solid, tangible world with the elusive 'seen' world of light and colour. He never separated the two spheres, as the Impressionists managed to do, but he gave both equal importance. Water appears in all forms in his work, from small shady rills to marshy, stagnant ponds, from vigorous flowing rivers to tranquil lakes – and however incidental its role in a composition might seem, for Daubigny it remained the principal focal point of his work.

CHARLES FRANÇOIS DAUBIGNY
THE VILLAGE STREAM, 1877
Metropolitan Museum of Art, New York

of the water, eddying beneath breezes or lapping from the hulls of boats, and to convey the thrust of the current beneath the surface, the enormous sculpting power which shapes so much of the landscape around us. The pictorial problems and advantages of reflected and refracted light, bouncing off the surface of the water while at the same instant passing through it, only adds to the peculiar visual properties which rivers have to offer.

One of the first great masters of French landscape painting in the nineteenth century, Jean Baptiste Camille Corot (1796–1875), seemed fascinated by rivers, and their appearance in his paintings provides a convenient metaphor to explain his position as a key transitional figure between the classical landscape painters and the Naturalist painters of the Barbizon school. Corot was born in Paris, and started his working life following in his father's footsteps in the drapery trade. He began his career as a painter in 1822, entering the studios of the classical painters Michallon and then Bertin. Here he became familiar with the classical formulae for developing landscape as a backdrop for figure studies.

In 1825 he went to Rome, where he painted many of the standard classical monuments and produced a major landscape which he exhibited in the Salon of 1827, *The Bridge at Narni*. These early paintings represent a high point in the informal classical landscape style and yet also mark the emergence of something quite new in French painting – a whole-hearted commitment to the pictorial qualities of paint and colour used instinctively as a means of representing the life and solidity of a real landscape. Where in classical painting composition is determined by a strict balance of forms, and colour is subservient to linear definition, Corot's approach showed a compositional sense determined by the forms of the landscape itself, a bright, fresh palette and a rejection of drawing in favour of modelling directly in paint. There is a clear and unaffected feeling to these early works, and they were to prove enormously influential.

However, certain basic characteristics of the classical landscape were retained in Corot's work: gentle diagonal planes were selected and emphasized as a means of establishing depth and recession (rivers and glimpsed areas of water were especially useful here); foreground features – trees or figures – were often carefully juxtaposed against middle- and background elements; the subject of his paintings – often a town, bridge or large building – tended to be set in the distant middleground which helped to give a sense of overall unity to the scene, cradled within its own landscape surroundings. The river motif, a central element in classical landscape painting (mainly due to its usefulness in introducing serpentine form and implying spatial depth) was the most prominent feature of his classical background which Corot carried over into his later style.

Corot was one of the first French painters to approach his native landscape on its own terms. He travelled widely in France, and produced many views of the Rhône, Loire, Oise and Seine. His importance in the development of French landscape painting was crucial (see South of Paris chapter).

Charles François Daubigny (1817–78) was a close friend of Corot, and admired his early Italian paintings. He too went to Italy, in 1836, and also travelled widely in the rest of Europe, visiting England, Holland and Spain. His father was a landscape painter in the domestic classical style, and at the age of 21 Daubigny entered the studio of the history painter Paul Delaroche where, despite a lack of sympathy with the subject matter, he gained a firm grounding in the Romantic use of colour.

Daubigny was, if anything, more fascinated by rivers and water than was Corot. Where the latter tended to use rivers as formal compositional elements and useful colouristic counterpoints to the sky, Daubigny was absorbed with capturing the ever-changing characteristics of water itself. This was the central feature of a body of work which shows (like Corot's) an uncomplicated and direct enjoyment of nature. He always painted *en plein air*, often from a boat, which he converted into a floating studio (a craft which gained some notoriety at the time). In this vessel he travelled widely on the rivers – notably the Oise, Marne and Seine – and canals of France.

This closeness to water and its peculiar luminosity was a major factor in his development of a key pre-Impressionist style. Daubigny was one of the first painters to treat light as an independent feature in his work: the dualism between the objects in the landscape, solid and concrete, and the way in which the effects of light and atmosphere modify visual perception of them is central to Daubigny's art. Where the Barbizon painters incontrovertibly painted the features of the landscape as solid objects, and the Impressionists painted them merely as ephemeral surfaces, reflective of light (and its manifestation in colour), Daubigny's work sits transitionally between the two. The presence of water in so many of his paintings indicates its appeal as a medium between the concrete world and the light which surrounds and enlivens it.

Daubigny's work displays a contemplative enjoyment of the subtlety of the natural world, an enjoyment easily grasped by all those who take pleasure in 'messing around in boats'. He eventually settled at Auvers-sur-Oise, one of those locations peculiar to France which seem to attract a great number and variety of artists; Daubigny was the first, and possibly his high standing

JEAN BAPTISTE COROT
THE BRIDGE AT MANTES,
1868–70
Louvre, Paris

among the following generation explains why we find Harpignies, Pissarro, Berthe Morisot, Cézanne, Van Gogh and Vlaminck all working there in the later decades of the nineteenth century.

Indeed Corot, too, worked there during his middle period, when he had developed a unique, rather Rococo manner; something of his classical background emerged again in the form of Arcadian idylls, landscapes at dusk with shepherds set among trees, but brought to life with a fresh and original delicacy in which the individual features became unified in a harmonious balance of pastel tones and a gentle disintegration of form which created a strongly poetic effect.

For the young Impressionists, as for Daubigny, water constituted an important and fascinating medium for observation and experiment. The key phase in the development of the Impressionist style was the period Renoir and Monet spent working together at La Grenouillère on the Seine, just downstream from Paris. The two painters had first met in Gleyre's studio in 1862, where their fellow students had included Bazille and the Englishman Alfred Sisley. Monet and Renoir thereafter painted frequently *en plein air*, developing the fresh, colourful, modern naturalism which marks their early styles. The experience of working intensely at La Grenouillère, a fashionable bathing and eating resort, in the summer of 1869 seems to have fused their ideas. The choice of location was no more than a variation on their predominant themes throughout the 1860s – it offered another opportunity to observe Parisians at leisure, in the

CAMILLE PISSARRO
VIEW OF THE SEINE, 1901
Private collection

open air – but here the water seems to have acquired paramount importance. The figures in Monet's work became indistinct cyphers, the trees remained out of focus, and the surface of the Seine, broken into rippling strokes of pure pigment, became the central feature of the paintings. Renoir found it more difficult to ignore his predominant interest in people, and figures in his work were often larger and afforded more detail. Both painters also began to recognize and attempt to capture the way in which the colours of objects, and of shadows, become subtly modified by reflected light and by neighbouring colours. They experimented with unconventional, broken brush strokes and began to apply pure primary colours next to their complementary colours. These paintings begin to address the problem of painting pure light in a radically new way, and the presence of water was the catalyst for these formative perceptions.

The immense steps that were taken by Monet and Renoir can be illustrated by comparison between their work and a canvas by Manet painted five years later. *Claude Monet in His Floating Studio* (1874), apart from giving us a good idea of the Impressionist at work, shows the difficulty which Manet had in assimilating his young colleague's achievements. Although the modelling here is considerably looser than was usual in Manet's work, the image is still dominated by shape and form and by the

PAUL SIGNAC
THE SEINE AT ASNIÈRES,
1885
Paris, Collection Signac

JEAN-LÉON GÉRÔME
THE POND AT ST C. . ., c.1895
Richard Green Collection, London

ingenious contrivance of the composition, rather than by the close or analytic observation of colour or light.

The Seine, of course, remains the river most closely associated with the Impressionists, linking their two characteristic landscapes, Paris and Normandy. A string of locations scattered along the huge double-hairpin loops which the river traces after it leaves the Bois de Boulogne are intimately associated with the Impressionist world: La Grande Jatte, Asnières, Epinay, Argenteuil, Chatou, La Grenouillère and Port Marly.

One of the group who most successfully and consistently pursued the tenets of Impressionism throughout his career was Alfred Sisley (1839–99). He lived all his working life on the banks of the rivers in and around Paris. He was born in Paris to English parents and had a comfortable, secure childhood and youth. He rejected a commercial career in favour of painting, and by 1862 was making regular trips to the countryside to paint with Renoir and Monet. He worked exclusively in landscape, and from about 1870 produced some of the most balanced and controlled works of the Impressionist group. His compositional sense never embraced the striking juxtapositions favoured by Manet, Monet, Renoir and Degas, but rather seemed to emphasize his principal interests – the sky and water, the raw materials of pure Impressionism. Indeed, he once said, 'I always begin a picture with the sky.' His sensitivity to the nuances of light was, until 1890, more subtle than Monet's, and he rarely went out of his way to capture the spectacular effects which Monet sought. Nor did he ever challenge traditional compositional form or the rules of perspective. Nevertheless, there was a great versatility to his technique which allowed him to capture shades of mood in quite contrasting ways. In this Sisley emerges as one of the most accomplished of his contemporaries, forsaking the rather limited and narrow-minded interests which characterize the mature works of Monet, Renoir and Pissarro for a more virtuoso ability to adapt his technique to his pictorial requirements.

His father's business collapsed in the wake of the Franco-Prussian war of 1870–71, and from that point on Sisley had to support himself from his painting. He died just before the real worth of Impressionist art began to be realized, leaving a large body of pictures of the Seine valley and Normandy (he rarely left the area and avoided the clamour of Paris) which build up a remarkable record of the changing face of the region throughout the seasons. A record for posterity it remains, as Paris was rapidly expanding and within decades tarmacadam roads, industrial progress and the ravages of war would transform the area completely.

The social life on the banks of the Seine immediately

downstream from Paris attracted, in the 1880s, the attention of a remarkable new talent, Georges Seurat (1859–91). He had absorbed many of the lessons of the Impressionists, not least their interest in the urban social world, and their conviction that light and colour could be analysed logically. Seurat, however, saw that this process of analysis could be placed on a more rational, and less instinctive, footing. Various other influences were also important – Delacroix's paintings, the writings of the colour theorist Chevreul and the aesthetic analyst Charles Henry, and of David Sutter, who had studied visual perception. Seurat developed a method of creating a painted image which relied on extremely refined modelling in colour; the colours were selected on the principle of breaking down the combined effect of light and reflected light into colour contrasts, applied in tiny adjacent *pointilliste* dabs of pigment, a style which came to be known as Divisionism. As with Daubigny, Renoir and Monet before him, Seurat saw the peculiar pictorial function a large body of water could have as a recognizable medium between the concrete world and the light which renders it visible. His shimmering but flat and carefully controlled effect was played off against a reduction of forms to pure, geometrical shapes (reminiscent of Poussin's classicism) and a highly disciplined and flattened sense of composition.

At the 1884 *Salon des Artistes Indépendants* Seurat exhibited his monumental *Bathers at Asnières*. Two years later, the few rough edges of this achievement were smoothed out in his masterpiece *La Grande Jatte*. Both pictures took as their theme the popular recreational pursuits of contemporary Parisians visiting riverside resorts immediately outside the capital, and both include a wealth of closely observed and witty detail. However, the treatment remains enormously detached, the ideas behind the picture taking precedence over any observed content. The great sense of life and vivacity which marks the pure Impressionists and the unbounded joy in nature of Corot and Daubigny are here nullified; the proliferation of detailed sketches and studies which Seurat made in preparing these pictures seemed to act as filters, washing away the artist's direct relationship with nature as he pursued an aesthetic ideal.

Seurat's work pointed a determined finger down the road to pure abstraction, and this was probably his intention – unlike Cézanne and Monet, who unwittingly inspired many twentieth-century abstract painters. In Seurat's work we can clearly see how those painterly techniques which were originated earlier in the century as a means of representing more accurately the splendour of the visible world could eventually lead in another direction – away from nature and towards artifice.

ALBERT MARQUET
VIEW ON THE RIVER MARNE, 1913
Art Moderne, Ville de Pais, Paris

The domestic landscape as an acceptable motif in French painting enjoyed a remarkably swift development. Mastery of the classical landscape form, of course, had been a pre-requisite of Academic training since the inception of the Ecole des Beaux Arts in the seventeenth century – although its appearance in formal works was usually relegated to the background of portraits, still-life or history paintings. The innovative painters in the first decades of the nineteenth-century – who approached the French landscape on its own terms – Michel, Huet and the Barbizon School – did not enjoy Academic approval until late in their careers, if ever. This was as much to do with their subject matter – the unadorned landscape – as with their unorthodox methods of painting. With the Impressionists, the landscape became a central motif – although they too failed to achieve acceptance by the artistic establishment. However, by the 1890s it is interesting to see that stalwart of Academic principles, Gérôme, turning his hand very successfully to a contemporary landscape (see page 82). What had become clear by the last quarter of the nineteenth century was that the landscape was not only here to stay, but was the major arena in which innovative and experimental work was taking place. By the time Marquet produced this work (right), several years after his Fauve phase had been toned down, the landscape ranked with figure studies and still-life as one of the triumvirate of accepted principal motifs in contemporary art.

THE MOUNTAINS

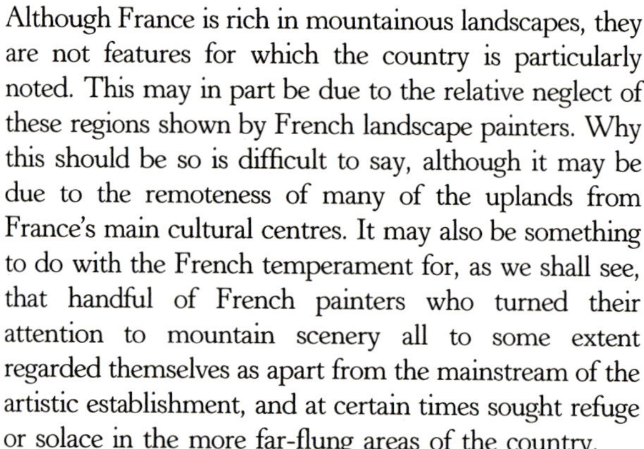

Although France is rich in mountainous landscapes, they are not features for which the country is particularly noted. This may in part be due to the relative neglect of these regions shown by French landscape painters. Why this should be so is difficult to say, although it may be due to the remoteness of many of the uplands from France's main cultural centres. It may also be something to do with the French temperament for, as we shall see, that handful of French painters who turned their attention to mountain scenery all to some extent regarded themselves as apart from the mainstream of the artistic establishment, and at certain times sought refuge or solace in the more far-flung areas of the country.

Four of France's five major mountain regions lie around her borders, and where they occur they determine the natural boundaries of the country. It would be wrong, however, to regard these ranges as much more than notional barriers. After all, Hannibal and his army scaled both the Pyrenees and the Alps *en route* to Rome in 220–218 BC. The Pyrenees failed to stop a number of Arab raiding parties from seriously threatening the Frankish empire in the eighth century AD, although the famous battle at Roncesvalles in the western passes in 778 finally put a stop to the invaders. During the Middle Ages one of Europe's most important pilgrimage routes, to the shrine at Santiago de Compostela in north-west Spain, led over these mountains; further north, a major branch of this route also picked its way through the Massif Central via such centres as Conques. Similarly, the Mont Cenis and Great St Bernard passes in the Alps formed the major overland commercial routes between Italy and northwest Europe throughout the Middle Ages, especially while the western Mediterranean remained a resort for Arab pirates and other freebooters (only later did the Swiss and Austrian passes come into use). In addition, the Alpine districts of Savoy, Dauphiné and Piedmont were so often bones of territorial contention that, although heavily depopulated in times of war, the higher valleys were constantly garrisoned and every village or strategic bluff was fortified.

In the north, the Jura region of Franche-Comté, too, was a continual area of dispute, fought over by the French kings and their Hapsburg and Bourbon rivals; it constituted a major staging-post in a complex chain of tactical holdings which allowed the Spanish monarchy to maintain an overland supply route to its army in

J M W TURNER
A COTTAGE DESTROYED BY AN AVALANCHE, 1810
Tate Gallery, London

◀ GUSTAVE COURBET
THE LOUE VALLEY, WITH A GATHERING STORM, 1870
Musée des Beaux-Arts, Strasbourg

GUSTAVE COURBET
"BONJOUR, M. COURBET!", 1854
Musée Fabre, Montpellier

Flanders during the Dutch Revolt of 1559–1648. Its acquisition by France in 1678 was a critical step in establishing the modern borders of France. The upland districts to the north, in Lorraine and the Ardennes, were also seen as natural barriers; their strategic advantage was seriously undermined, however, in 1870 when the Prussian army thrust into France via Metz and Sedan; 70 years later armoured Panzer divisions again took France by surprise when they broke through the Ardennes forest, bypassing the elaborate fortifications of the Maginot Line.

Despite their dubious qualities as strategic barriers, the Pyrenees and the Alps and, more recently, the Jura and the uplands of the north-east have traditionally marched with the political borders of France; like many border regions, each retains a cultural character distinct from that of the French heartland. This is also true of the other great upland area, the Massif Central, whose remote fastnesses, despite the erection of innumerable medieval castles and later châteaux, have fostered a strong sense of individual locality.

Mountains have always attracted landscape painters. The largely fanciful landscape backdrops of many medieval paintings tend to include imaginary mountains and unlikely crags. Such features are, of course, more eye-catching than flat plains, but within a composition they can serve a specific purpose: a recession of peaks, one overlapping another, provides a simple device for creating an illusion of space and distance. Furthermore, the peculiar atmospheric conditions and luminosity associated with higher altitudes constitute a ready-made colour scheme whereby tonal recession to a distant horizon can be easily conveyed: the northern European painters of the fifteenth and sixteenth centuries developed a palette in which a rich brocade of foreground colours blended into yellows and greens in the middle distance, yielding in turn to a variety of brisk azure tints towards the horizon. Distant mountains provided a motif which exploited this rich format to best effect. They also added a dimension of the exotic to representations of action and landscape which were rarely conceived to be regarded as real, but rather as miraculous or fantastic.

It is impossible to identify accurately the mountains found in these early landscape paintings. The sharply pinnacled crenellations which are to be seen in, say, the work of the Limbourg brothers (see Introduction), although probably based on first-hand experience of mountains, remain, like so much else in their work, a distillation of that experience, idealized and made more fantastic in the service of pictorial effect.

Mountains feature prominently within the tradition of classical landscape painting. Here they are gentler than their medieval forebears, more in keeping with the notion of classical proportion and sublime harmony, but no more real for all that. Claude Lorraine certainly made sketches of the gentle Alban hills behind Rome, and used these in his work; but he increasingly sought out or invented elaborate rock forms which, like Poussin, he could work up into elements which more closely complemented his pictorial designs than reality itself. For many of their followers, of course, the physical experience of visiting Italy – a basic qualification for any painter aspiring to classical credibility – actually involved crossing the Alps. The Alps, however, did not appeal to their sensibilities or match their training and aims: the mountains were too massive, too rugged, and too fraught with unsettling hazards – rockfalls, blizzards, uncomfortable snowbound nights and (until the mid-nineteenth century) bands of brigands – to fit with their notions of tranquillity and balance.

The most notable views of French mountains, especially of the Jura and the Alps, were produced by English Grand Tourists *en route* to Italy during the eighteenth and nineteenth centuries. Sir Alexander Cozens and his son John Robert, two of the most influential English topographic watercolourists, seized upon this spectacular upland scenery with relish, and later Turner could not resist the opportunity to confront nature at its most sublime (characteristically marrying it to a sense of historical grandeur) in *Snow Storm: Hannibal and his Army crossing the Alps* (1812).

However, these dramatic qualities do not seem to have appealed to their French contemporaries, and it is not until well into the nineteenth century that the peculiar topographic qualities and pictorial potential of mountain scenery begin to appear in the work of native artists.

Gustave Courbet (1819–77) was born of peasant stock in the small town of Ornans in the southern Jura; he began to paint while studying law at Besançon. Among his first important works were *L'Après Diner à Ornans* (1844) and *Funeral at Ornans* (1850). Both pictures self-consciously draw on his particular provincial background for their subject matter. The application of paint is rough and their composition careful but unpretentious: the latter canvas masses a frieze of sombre mourners against solid blocks of rock escarpment in the distance. The forthright style and uncritical presentation of everyday life in the countryside in both works was designed to shock the sensibilities of the Parisian aesthetes. His notorious presentation of rude country folk, warts and all, provided Courbet with, on the one hand, the sobriquet of 'Realist' painter, and on the other with the means to pursue the type of pure landscape painting which formed much of his output in the 1860s.

In 1855, when 2 of 12 canvases he had submitted for the *Exposition Universelle* in Paris were rejected, Courbet staged an independent show outside the exhibition gate, under the banner 'The Pavilion of Realism'. Among the 43 canvases he exhibited was *The Artist's Studio* (1855), an allegory in which the conflict between the brash anti-intellectual painter from the provinces and the cultivated Parisian *cognoscenti* is exposed. The painting combines portraits of writers such as Baudelaire, Champfleury and the socialist philosopher Proudhon, with various symbolic figures: Truth (a child) and Innocence (a female nude, ostensibly an artist's model). A huntsman and rustic labourers also crowd the studio. At the centre of this bizarre gathering sits Courbet himself, painting a mountainous landscape. The walls of the *atèlier* are hung with landscapes of his native region. The work was unavoidably a 'statement' in the grand manner. It demonstrated Courbet's ability to produce the kind of complex, large-scale figurative composition which society then regarded as high art; in the same breath it simply stated Courbet's commitment to a new kind of landscape painting which he regarded as of equal if not greater worth.

Following the *succès de scandale* of this exhibition, Courbet increasingly turned to painting landscapes, and in the early 1860s he often worked with Monet and Whistler on the Channel coast (see Normandy chapter). But it is the canvases produced in his native region which provide the clearest summary of Courbet's concerns.

Approached from the west, the Jura mountains grow from a series of rises above the river valleys of the Saône and Doubs towards the rich vine-growing region around Aubois. Beyond this are the mountains themselves, a series of volcanic folds which eventually give way on the east to the lakes of Geneva and Neuchâtel. The range is dissected by numerous fast-flowing trout streams which have cut ravines in the rock, forming cool, conifer-clad valleys. Rich in game and in local craft activity, the meagre opportunities for earning a living in this wild landscape seem summed up in Courbet's famous paintings of local stonebreakers.

Courbet's approach to painting this landscape seems

GUSTAVE COURBET
THE MOUNTAIN HUT, c.1860
Galeria d'Arte Moderna, Turin

JEAN-FRANÇOIS MILLET
IN THE AUVERGNE (THE MOUNTAIN PASTURE), 1867–69
Art Institute of Chicago

itself to grow from the subject matter. He applied pigment in rough, broad strokes, laying paint on thickly, often with a palette knife, as if modelling or rebuilding the landscape. This created a sense of blockiness and weight which complemented his close observation of the tectonic structure of the landforms in front of him. Courbet often ignored the traditional technique of organizing spatial recession – moving from a sharply defined foreground through a series of receding planes to a distant horizon – in favour of a series of monumental middle-ground masses which block off the distant view. These are held together by the play of light and shade, and dynamic tension – that which excites the eye and absorbs the onlooker – would be established by employing either features of sharply contrasting size or, as in *The Dying Stag* (1861), figures and animals in violent action. In the absence of people, the thick forest and serried cliffs of the high Jura served Courbet as a source for pure landscape.

Towards the end of the 1860s, the central motifs in the last paintings he was to complete in the region became less solid. Figures diminish in size, stone cottages no longer appear, and the blocks of cliff and rock lose their prominence as the dark interiors of the timbered valleys spread over his canvases. At a time when Impressionist painters were searching for ever more light and colour, Courbet's brushwork sought to reconstitute in paint the mysterious absence of light and dense foliage of the sunless forest.

Courbet began his career with a 'message', the urge to make a public statement. He ended it caught up in an intensely personal struggle to combine truth to nature with the desire to create a complete illusion in paint, to blend the act of seeing with the act of painting. The arena for this struggle was the high Jura; for the reclusive Courbet, his native landscape provided a familiar and unique subject. Here he could paint undisturbed, in an environment which provided an endless variety of dramatic natural forms, colours and light effects. It is more than a coincidence that a mountain – Mont Ste Victoire in Provence – would be a recurring motif for Cézanne in his similarly solitary quest a generation later (see Provence chapter).

The other great figure of the French Realist school, Jean François Millet (1814–75), also of peasant birth, worked mainly in his native Normandy and in Barbizon (see Normandy and South of Paris chapters). In the summers of 1866, 1867 and 1868 he accompanied his wife on visits to the spa town of Vichy in the northern Auvergne which were recommended for her health. These brief sojourns produced a large number of drawings and sketches, some of which were later worked up into oil paintings or pastels. Millet's work concentrated on the emotive appeal of the working life of the peasant. His landscape backgrounds are usually flat plains, contributing to the feeling of stark monumentality he wished to achieve. Millet's experience of the Auvergne brought surprising results. The region is notable even today for its relative remoteness. Although well stocked with manors and chateaux to the north and west, it was not until nineteenth-century industrialism began to exploit the minerals and ores found in abundance in the limestone strata in the heart of the Massif Central that the area was at all opened up. Communications and settlement remain limited due to the difficult terrain, and on the broad shoulders of the mountains in the north and east farmers earn a sparse living rearing livestock – sheep, goats and, where possible, dairy cattle, penned into fields bounded by low stone walls. On the southern face of the outcrop, the Languedoc, a richer, seasonal sheep-herding economy developed: bred in the warmer lowlands of the Mediterranean hinterland, the flocks are driven up the slopes to the cooler pastures in the summer. To the west existence is more precarious. Here the plateau is deeply incised by a number of rivers forming gorges which today enjoy a considerable tourist appeal, but which in the past made the life and work of the upland farmer a difficult one.

During Millet's first stay – his longest, with four weeks at Vichy and a week travelling near Clermont-Ferrand and Mont-Dore – he admitted that the area reminded him of his childhood in Normandy. By this time both Normandy and Barbizon were becoming popular short-trip resorts from Paris. In the Auvergne the winding sunken lanes, the isolated farmsteads and the simple everyday life of the peasants brought about a period of nostalgia. *The Mountain Pasture* (1867–69) is substantially different from Millet's major works produced elsewhere: the horizon is high, allowing a simple enjoyment in painting the flowers and grasses of the upland pasture to suffuse the canvas, an effect complemented by the studied simplicity of the peasant girl and her cows. There is no hint of the contrived monumentality of his better-known works, and it thus remains a refreshing and uncomplicated view of a disappearing rural life.

The effect of the mountain scenery of Provence upon Cézanne and Van Gogh is examined elsewhere (see

CHAIM SOUTINE
VIEW OF CÉRET, c.1922
Baltimore Museum of Art

Provence chapter), but the influence of their work on an artist of the next generation was to produce some of the most extraordinary landscape paintings of the twentieth century. Chaim Soutine (1893–1943) was born in Lithuania and came to Paris in 1913. Beset by an unusual degree of self-doubt, and with a morbid fear of exhibiting his work, his career nevertheless successfully encompassed all the major themes of modern representational art – still-life, portraiture, the figure and the landscape. In Paris he fell in with a group of expatriate *peintres maudites*, including Modigliani and Chagall. He also saw the works of Rembrandt, El Greco and Tintoretto in the Louvre. From these he acquired a powerful approach to colour and texture, and an understanding of the emotive power of paint itself. He used these stylistic tools in a manner which was vigorous and direct. Always working in the presence of the subject, he strove to capture in paint, in a single sitting, the total range of emotions stirred within him. This approach courted the obvious danger of loss of control. Soutine solved this hazard by his careful modulation of colour; he seems to have absorbed something of the careful compositional balance of colour found in Cézanne's work.

In Paris his main preoccupations were psychologically penetrating and emotionally disturbing portraits, or still-life studies of rotting carcases, painted under appalling conditions. However, he spent two lengthy periods working outside the city, at Céret, near Perpignan in the Pyrenees, from 1919–22, and at Cagnes in eastern Provence from 1925. The latter period has obvious geographical connections with Cézanne and with Van Gogh; indeed, Soutine's approach to painting and his finished work is reminiscent of the Dutchman's (although Soutine openly dismissed Van Gogh's work), but this similarity first came into focus at Céret. Here he concentrated for the first time on landscape painting, and here he effectively established his style.

The eastern Pyrenees, looking northwards over the dry vine-clad slopes and stony hills of Corbières and Roussillon, retain a uniquely regional, almost autonomous, flavour. The population is really Catalan, sharing a sense of nationality with their immediate neighbours across the Pyrenees; the fertile plain around Perpignan is one of the oldest and richest agricultural regions of France, specializing in early and exotic vegetables and fruit. The terracotta tile roofs of the buildings and the clear Mediterranean air, together enlivening the delicate browns and greens of the countryside, found an odd interpreter in Soutine, and yet it is not difficult to appreciate the impact of the bright light and colour on his northern eye.

Soutine's early works at Céret are immensely distorted, indeed they are distressing to look at. He employed the diagonal thrust (usually from lower left to upper right) favoured by Van Gogh as a means of organizing the elements of the landscape, albeit creating a vertiginous sensation as figures, trees, boulders and lanes appear to be sucked into an upward surge of paint and brushwork. It is surprising in a style so expressionistic to find that Soutine's palette is remarkably limited: the landscapes tend to be constructed around yellows and greens. It is likely that this was a direct result of observing the landscape before him. Certainly the mountainous setting around the ancient town of Céret offered other formal advantages: the horizon could be very high, allowing most of the canvas to be taken up with vigorous rendering of detail. Indeed, the skyline is often so high as to be almost indistinguishable, and below it the sharp inclines and deep valley perspectives lent themselves to strong diagonal compositions. Where most landscape painting is predominantly horizontal in format, Soutine's elements are often organized in an impassioned series of near verticals.

The impact of the Pyrenees upon Soutine was nothing short of dramatic. His experiences there provided a confidence which permeated his later work. The stay in Provence was regenerative rather than innovatory, and after the Nazi occupation of northern France in 1940 Soutine escaped persecution as a Jew by seeking refuge in the Pyrenees, where he died from an ulcer in 1943.

For Soutine, like Courbet and Cézanne before him, the mountain landscapes of France offered a unique opportunity to work, in relative isolation, at a largely personal problem concerning the relationship between nature, the artist and paint. The motifs were larger than life, as were the problems these painters set themselves. As so often when artists are confronted by nature at its most awesome, the final impression they leave us tells us more about the men behind the canvas than the scenery before them.

NORMANDY

Normandy, the agriculturally rich region which straddles the lower reaches of the great rivers which flow through the Ile de France, is one of the best-known and best-loved areas of France outside Paris. This is partly due to its many historical associations with the English-speaking world, and partly due to the many and varied representations of the area by innumerable artists over the last two centuries.

For our purposes we will consider Normandy as that section of the French coast which rises from the northern flank of the Breton peninsula at Avranches; sweeps round the north-facing granite block of the Cherbourg peninsula; and then flattens out to form a series of long, flat sandy beaches reaching north to the border with Belgium, beaches broken by occasional downland cliffs and the estuaries of the Seine and the Somme. The hinterland of this long coastline stretches in the south just beyond the watershed with the Loire basin (formed by a low ridge below which are scattered Laval, Le Mans and Chartres), east towards the Ile de France and Paris, and in the north rolls across the gentle undulations of Picardy and Artois to the open expanses of Flanders.

The alluvial soils deposited by the meandering rivers, the arteries of the region, overlay a mixture of chalk and loamy clay, a wonderfully fertile foundation for temperate mixed agriculture. The wooded slopes which curtain the south of Normandy overlook a dense patchwork of village, orchard and pasture which stretches continuously to the Low Countries. Only the Cherbourg peninsula, with its often marshy northern foreshore and bushy *bocage* ground cover, breaks this pattern. The lush meadows and chalky downland pastures support some of the richest dairy farming in Europe, Normandy butter being at least as famous as the locally-produced Camembert cheese. Normandy is one of the few areas of France not noted so much for wine as for beverages produced from the overspill of the limitless apple orchards – cider and the unique Norman apple liqueur, Calvados.

In addition to the great agricultural resources of Normandy are the fisheries, exploited from its coastal ports – unfortunately less notable now since the demarcation of international fishing rights in the waters of the Channel, North Sea and the northern Atlantic brought into existence long-range trawling fleets; nevertheless, the restaurants of the Norman seaboard are among the most noted in Europe for their *fruits de mer*.

JEAN-FRANÇOIS MILLET
PEASANT COTTAGE AT GRUCHY, 1854–73
Rijksmuseum Kröller-Müller, Otterlo

This fine example of Boudin's unique style makes clear the debt owed him by the Impressionists. The principal thrust of his style is towards fixing in paint the subtle nuances of colour and light peculiar to the sea-shore. It is also reminiscent in many ways of the way in which small figures were used anecdotally in Flemish and Dutch landscape painting two centuries beforehand. This trait persisted in the work of many Impressionists – Pissarro especially. Nevertheless, Boudin's more important single contribution to Impressionist technique was his iack of regard for realistic representation in favour of breaking the surface of his work up into carefully balanced paint-marks, which only came together as a whole to form the composition. The attention paid to a corner of the sky or to the immediate foreground of the beach is as great as that expended on the figures and boats of the middle-distance. It was this feature, and his peculiar ability to render light, which would so impress the young Monet.

EUGÉNE BONDIN
THE JETTY AT DEAUVILLE,
1869
Louvre, Paris

Historically the region prospered, like Provence and the Rhône valley in the south-west, from its position at one of Europe's major crossroads for trade, commerce and communication.

The Seine provided Paris with a lifeline to the Channel, the Atlantic and the North Sea, and the flow of commerce from the capital to the western coast provided a huge income. It is also the closest point on the European continent to the British Isles and, although the relationship between Britain and France has not always been a happy one, the scale of revenues accrued from links across the Straits of Dover has often been substantial for both countries.

Strategically Normandy was vital, commanding the eastern coastline of the Channel and the Straits of Dover, still one of the world's busiest waterways. Control of this maritime bottleneck has often been a key to power; its potential was recognized by the Vikings from Denmark, who set up colonies and trading posts on both sides of the Channel, and it was these Norsemen who gave Normandy its name. The Viking, or Norman, kingdom on the French side of the Channel grew steadily more powerful and, finding its expansionist urges blocked inland, launched the great invasion of England in 1066, inaugurating a cross-Channel empire which lasted, in one form or another, until the English finally relinquished power over French territory in 1453, although Calais remained in English hands until 1558. Some of the earliest 'views' of Normandy date from the Hundred Years' War (1337–1453) between England and France, and illustrate the events of the long struggle. These illuminations sometimes emphasize the agriculturally rich countryside outside the heavily fortified Channel ports such as Calais – the prize for the victor. Often, however, they convey the appalling devastation and laying waste of both town and country which was the hallmark of many of the campaigns.

Conversely, gaining control of the Channel coast and its ports was one of the essential keynotes of power for the Valois monarchs of the French High Middle Ages, for since the twelfth century two major trading networks had grown up in north-west Europe, both of which relied greatly upon Normandy as a gateway to the principal river and overland routes to the south. The extensive trading pattern throughout Scandinavia and the Baltic region flowed around the Jutland peninsula and south to the Channel, finding landfall at the Norman and Belgian ports. Further, the Hansa trading league of northern Europe linked the wool producers of England and Germany with the manufacturing and trading centres in Flanders, immediately north of Normandy, and Normandy profited from the southward thrusts of this economic net. Something of the wealth of Normandy during the Middle Ages can be gauged by the proliferation of rich architecture – especially Gothic churches and cathedrals – which survive to this day, for example at Amiens, Rouen, Beauvais and Chartres.

With the recovery of Normandy from English hands – the prime French gain from the Hundred Years' War – the region became, and continued to be, strategically and economically crucial to the French economy. Its strategic value came into focus very clearly twice in the twentieth century. The Somme offensive on the Western Front in 1916 and the Normandy landings of D-Day in June 1944 both represent nadirs of modern man's capacity to wage total war; for both Allied and German survivors the occasions were unforgettable nightmares, but the French people and landscapes bore the real brunt of sheer destruction. The cities of Amiens and Caen have now both been rebuilt, but their modernity is an emblematic reminder of the cost of war.

The first painters to record the Norman landscape in any accurate detail were from the immediately adjacent Low Countries and from England. For the latter this was understandable; it was the first region of 'the Continent' most English travellers would encounter. For Belgians and Dutchmen, Normandy was a neighbouring region, differentiated from their native countries only by an invisible political border.

The Anglo-French exchange of ideas, which largely inaugurated the blossoming of French landscape painting in the second quarter of the nineteenth century (see Introduction), began some years earlier. The writer Chateaubriand had written favourably of what he had observed of the English landscape tradition during his visit to England in 1795; Thomas Girtin, fellow student of Turner, painted views of Paris in 1801; Crome, John Glover, Frederick Cox and John Sell Cotman all exhibited at the Paris Salon, and de Loutherbourg, Delacroix and Géricault visited England. Richard Parkes Bonington (1802–28) went to Paris in 1815 and spent most of his remaining 13 years in France; his application of the English watercolour and topographic tradition to the French landscape was highly influential. The common factor in all these journeys and exchanges was Normandy, which had to be crossed laboriously by coach or riverboat in order to reach the Channel ports from Paris. Further, the Norman landscape as it approaches the coast is only distinguishable from that of the Sussex and Kentish shores by virtue of differences in architectural styles and agricultural techniques. It shared the same muddy skies and the same rolling downland, breached at the seashore by cliffs. Thus, after the resounding impact of the exhibition of Constable's paintings in Paris in

1824, many of those painters who wished to emulate the English tradition naturally turned to Normandy as an ideal setting. It was also the nearest area of the French coast to Paris, and this was important, as seascapes and coastal views were popular subjects in the English landscape tradition – and had played an even larger part in the older Dutch landscape school.

Eugène Fromentin, in his lengthy appreciation of the Dutch and Flemish schools, *Masters of Past Time* (1875), acknowledged that although the influence of the Netherlands' landscapists upon the development of the nineteenth-century French school was considerable, it was difficult to cite any actual evidence. Certainly in the early works of Corot and Rousseau we see a turning away from Italianate and classical landscape formulae in favour of a more direct and honest approach to painting the landscape; also we can see to some extent a rejection of those features of the landscape which are more closely associated with the classical school – mountains, meandering rivers, foreground and middleground framing elements, golden sunsets – in favour of those more conspicuously associated with the Dutch school – rain-sodden fields, cloudy skies, flat agricultural plains and distant level horizons. Again, Normandy was eloquently suited for the study of such features, and so we begin to see painters working in Normandy at the same time as a kind of Northern aesthetic began to emerge.

One aspect of this Northern aesthetic can be found in the work of the novelist Victor Hugo. His books often embraced a feel for Gothicism, and his watercolours of Paris, Luxembourg and, after settling in the Channel Islands, of Jersey and Normandy, are rather fantastical views tinged with a Northern medievalism.

Among the first major painters to work in Normandy was Eugène Isabey (1803–86) whose numerous seascapes, worked in wonderfully relaxed, loose brushstrokes and a tastefully muted pastel palette, set the tone for a special sub-genre of seascape – the breezy day, with small boats under sail. Boudin, Monet, Manet, Renoir and Signac all turned their hand to this motif, with greatly varying results. Isabey's ability to capture the feeling of wind and wave, of sunlight dancing on moving water, of fleeting natural effects frozen in time, sets him somewhere between Constable and the Impressionists. His touch was lighter than the former, and on the whole more successful than the latter (who often relied on the uncomfortable veracity and distortion revealed by fast-exposure photography to capture a feeling of movement). Isabey's style is, by contrast, not analytic but instinctive, determined more by a genuine knowledge of, and passion for, sailing boats and the life of the sea shore than by abstract artistic notions.

CLAUDE MONET
THE TERRACE AT SAINTE-ADDRESSE, 1866
Metropolitan Museum of Art, New York

Isabey's landscapes and seascapes enjoyed great success at his debut in the 1824 Salon. He went on to be one of the contributors to the *Voyages pittoresques et romantiques dans l'ancienne France* (published 1820–78), a project which was influenced by English antiquarianism and view series such as those produced by the Daniell brothers and Turner. Other contributors included the antiquarian view-painter Horace Vernet, the architect Viollet-le-Duc, Félix Ziem, who specialized in classi-

cal ruins, and Bonington. It was an important step towards the development of a topographic tradition in French painting.

Among Isabey's pupils were two painters, Eugène Boudin and Johan Barthold Jongkind, whose work in Normandy shows a concern with the painterly qualities of topographic Naturalism, qualities which would lead to the development of Impressionism.

The work of Eugène Boudin (1824–98) appears superficially similar to that of Isabey. A closer examination reveals rather more pronounced technical qualities which were to be immensely influential upon the next generation of artists. Notable both as a graphic draughtsman (he numbered Daumier among his studio assistants) and as an inventive colourist (Monet was a pupil), Boudin's offshore views from Honfleur and Le Havre and the beaches of Trouville (which became a highly fashionable resort) prefigure directly in technique the concerns of the Impressionists. Boudin's style was informal and sketchy. His reduction of form to distant, delicate notations of colour within a bright setting provided the basis for Impressionist technique; his liking for the luminosity of the reflected light of the sea shore, and his taste for the bustle and colour of the fashionable élite at leisure, also endeared him to the next generation. He exhibited at the first Impressionist exhibition in 1874.

Johan Barthold Jongkind (1819–91) was born in Holland, and was persuaded to visit France in 1846 by Isabey. Thereafter he worked regularly in his native country and in Paris and Normandy. His delicate watercolour studies and drawings of marine views and the ports of Normandy were made from nature, and his oil paintings worked up from these in the studio. It is remarkable, therefore, that he captured the play of light and delicate nuances of air and atmosphere so successfully. Jongkind exhibited with the Barbizon group. His work was much admired by the young Monet, and by the critics Baudelaire and the Goncourt brothers, although his life was spent in poverty and squalor. Later he lived near Grenoble, where alcoholism and mental instability dogged him, as they did Van Gogh.

In this early work by Monet, the influence of Boudin is clear, as are some of the fundamental aspects of Monet's perception which would carry him through the 1860s to the development of full Impressionism. The canvas is very evenly painted, with equal attention to detail in all parts. There is a certain looseness of technique which, added to more obvious features such as the fluttering flag and streams of smoke on the horizon, convey a sense of immediacy, whilst simultaneously reminding us that we are looking at a painting rather than an accurate representation of a scene. The composition, like Boudin's, is organized in horizontal places of recession – there is little evidence here of the Japanese compositional influence which would be a hallmark of his style in later years.

JOHAN BARTHOLD JONGKIND
THE BEACH AT SAINTE-ADDRESSE, 1863
Louvre, Paris

► EDOUARD MANET
THE ROADSTEAD AT BOULOGNE, 1863
Art Institute, Chicago

If Paris was the gravitational centre of the Impressionist movement, and if the lower reaches of the Seine outside Paris constitute the typical landscape of Impressionism, it is fair to say that Normandy was the birthplace of this most famous and popular of modern art movements. For it was here, at Le Havre in 1872, that Claude Monet painted *Impression: Sunrise* which, when exhibited in 1874, was picked on derisively to name the whole movement.

Monet (1840–1926) was born in Paris but raised in Le Havre, where in his youth he was encouraged by Boudin to paint landscapes *en plein air*, a habit in which he persisted all his life. He studied in Paris from 1859 at the *Atelier Suisse*, and there met Camille Pissarro. Following two years in Algeria with the army, he returned to Le Havre, where he met Jongkind, and subsequently went to Paris to work in the studio of Gleyre, there meeting Renoir, Sisley and Bazille. He painted with them at Barbizon, but travelled to Normandy again in 1864 to paint with Courbet; the next year they repeated the trip accompanied by Whistler, and in 1866 Monet worked there with Edouard Manet. This roll-call of the outstanding names of late nineteenth-century French painting gives some indication of the heady atmosphere in which Monet worked, and throws considerable light on his subsequent development.

During this period the dominant vogue was for Realism, with its emphasis on honesty to nature and truth to subject matter. Courbet, the outstanding Realist, had already begun to question the way in which visual veracity could be achieved in paint; he was developing an impasto style in which the flecks of paint which emerge from, or are laid over, a welter of heavy pigment create both a feeling of immense structural solidity and of effervescent light; his seascapes of Normandy show creamy, solid swathes of foam, cresting turbulent waves breaking beneath palpable mounds of cloud. Manet, in contrast, was applying to landscape motifs his style of painting in flat tonal areas of colour. These pictures often feel similar to the work of Jongkind, although his graphic style is, if anything, looser; in his depictions of sailing boats in, for example, *The Roadstead at Boulogne* (1863) we are aware of his primary concern with the picture as a painting rather than a view, a carefully conceived interaction of forms embedded on the canvas in a series of chromatic layers. By the late 1860s, probably due to his experience of painting landscapes, Manet's palette was becoming brighter, and his forms were increasingly enlivened by the modelling effects of light and local colour, features central to Impressionism.

It is in Monet's work, however, that the landscape of Normandy acquires its most characteristic pictorial 'look' in the popular imagination. This is partly due to the sheer number of paintings Monet produced there. He worked mainly in and around Paris until the Franco-Prussian war of 1870, and then escaped to England with Pissarro for two years; returning to Paris in 1872, he was based just outside the capital, at Argenteuil, until 1878 – years which can be said to be formative in his career (see North of Paris chapter). Throughout this period he often visited Normandy, and in 1883 he settled at Giverny, on the Seine, midway between Paris and the Normandy coast. An early painting such as *Snow-covered road at Honfleur* (1865) shows the various influences of Jongkind (choice of subject and composition), Courbet (in the vigorous brushwork) and Manet (in the flat tonal

manet

CLAUDE MONET
IMPRESSION: SUNRISE, 1872
Musée Marmottan, Paris

This picture gave its name to the first movement of modern art quite incidentally. Listed as a variation in the catalogue for the first Impressionist exhibition of 1874, the term was seized upon, and transmuted into a general title of derision. It was also, as it turned out, a very accurate title. Painted at dawn in the harbour at Le Havre, Monet had merely wished to capture the essential elements of the scene in his own unique way – figurative details being subordinate to the combination of light and atmospheric conditions as the sun rose through the morning mist. Nevertheless, when compared to the *ébauche* style of oil sketch (see Michel: The Storm, page 56) it is clear that Monet has introduced structural and controlling elements, derived from his work with Renoir at La Grenouillère and from Japanese prints, which mean that he has little to add to the picture. Monet's 'search for true tone' was methodical but instinctive. When set beside Seurat's more rational, scientific Divisionist style (right) of fourteen years later the painterly qualities of Monet's manner became clear. Divisionism represented in a sense, the death of Impressionism in that it eradicated the intuitive impulse, and made the search for truth to nature artificial and stilted.

GEORGES SEURAT
BEACH AT BAS-BUTIN, 1886
Musée des Beaux Arts, Tournai

approach to colour). By the time of *Impression: Sunrise* (1872) his work with Renoir at la Grenouillère (see North of Paris chapter), and with Pissarro in London (where he saw Turner's canvases) had brought about a substantial change. Firstly, he was now concentrating purely on landscapes; secondly, in this work the forms of the ships, cranes and quays of the harbour at Le Havre have lost all sense of solidity and merge into an atmospheric mass of sky and water suffused with the deep red of the rising sun. Too much should not be read into this work; its title originally indicated that it was a sketch rather than a finished painting. Monet exhibited the canvas because no reworking or more finished version could convey as successfully the effect he sought.

This disintegration of form is a hallmark of Monet's above all other Impressionists. He became fascinated by the way in which light is made visible by colour, and made palpable by the objects in its way. Atmospheric conditions – mists and hazes – were of particular interest to him, and after seeing Turner's work he altogether abandoned traditional linear perspective, establishing depth purely through accurately observed aerial perspective (the way in which shapes, contours and colours become less distinct and begin to merge the further they are from the eye). In following this path of development, Monet realized that he needed to seek subjects which would provide him with enough pictorial form to anchor a style which, although highly naturalistic and dependent

CAMILLE PISSARRO
ILE LACROIX, ROUEN, 1888
Private collection

on the close observation of nature, would be in great danger of seeming increasingly abstract. The seashore of Normandy, and that of Brittany (see Brittany chapter), provided him with ideal monumental natural shapes. The coast at Etrétat, just north of Le Havre, was a favourite subject. Here the sea has created arches and blow-holes in the chalk cliffs, which rise sheer from the water. These great natural forms provided a wonderfully solid foil for Monet's delicate treatment of sunlight and also allowed him to address the traditional problem of rendering water in violent movement. His solution was utterly convincing, and in the studies of waves smashing against the foot of the cliffs and breaking through the great natural arches there is a splendid feel for the turbulence and destructive power of the sea.

Through the 1880s Monet returned again and again to the same landscape subjects, the better to study them under different light and atmospheric conditions and at different times of day. By the end of the decade and into the 1890s a more definite group of themes was emerging – his *Poplars*, *Haystacks* and *Rouen Cathedral* series. These subjects were not apparently linked by any particular formal similarities, but they do seem to sum up the essence of Normandy itself, the region which Monet loved and which, after settling at Giverny, he rarely left.

The long, straight, poplar-lined country roads so characteristic of this part of France provided Monet with a series of motifs in which the representation of aerial perspective could be quite knowingly set against the natural recession of the avenues of trees. In the 1890s the geometric structure provided by the tall trees afforded a framework for increasingly extreme orchestrations of pastel colours – compositions which veered towards abstraction. The play of light through these strangely shaped and sparsely clothed trees also held an obvious attraction for him.

The paintings of haystacks present quite a different aspect of his work. The forms of the stacks themselves, created by the pitching together of the mown and dried hay into large cylindrical stooks with conical crests to allow the worst of the weather to run off, were simple but immensely solid shapes. Their circular contours were ideal surfaces for displaying the varying fall of light. The stacks are usually presented within a simple landscape comprising three or four broad horizontal bands – the foreground field, middle ground hedgerow and houses, a distant rise of hills, and the sky. These repeated studies of the same motif in varying conditions and at different times of day were a logical outcome of Monet's interest in capturing specific instances. The strong contrasts in colour and focus which can be found in the series

Camille Pissarro, one of the more adventurous of the Impressionist painters, turning his hand to new techniques and ideas with an open mind, was one of the few of the older generation among the group capable of making pictorial sense of Seurat's Divisionist technique. He adopted the *pointilliste* style central to Divisionism in the mid-1880s, and soon turned it to his own ends, rejecting the programmatic system for selecting colours espoused by Seurat in favour of a more intuitive approach. The results, as here, are less rigid and statuesque than Seurat's paintings, creating rather a synthesis of the experience of light on the canvas. The influence of photography, the chemical reaction of sensitive emulsions when exposed to light, was of crucial importance to the scientific thought behind Divisionism. Pissarro here has created a tonal essay similar in effect to that of a photographic plate, but modified by the intrusion of the artists own sensibility in interpreting the scene before him. The way in which certain elements retain their hard edges, whilst others blend with shadows or adjacent objects, the merging of sky and water, the delicate manner in which the plume of smoke dissipates into the atmosphere, all contribute strong tensions between the solid and the ethereal in the composition – pictorial depth and structure being maintained by the simple diagonal recessions around which the elements of the picture are organized.

perfectly illustrate his point; they convey the immense possibilities offered to the landscape painter if he is both observant and persistent. The range of variations Monet drew from a single motif, however, led to a point where the subject itself became unimportant. Some years later, the abstract painter Kandinsky remarked that the *Haystack* series made him aware of 'the unsuspected power of the palette, which surpassed all my dreams ... At the same time, unconsciously the object was discredited as an indispensable element of the picture.'

The Gothic façade of the cathedral at Rouen, the capital of Normandy just downstream from Monet's home, by contrast with both *Poplars* and *Haystacks* denied any opportunities for establishing more than a minimal pictorial depth. This massive slab of monumental masonry, highly textured and richly carved, built from the beautifuly grained and coloured Caen sandstone (and not, at that time, begrimed by the effects of industrial pollution), fronts a fairly modest open *place*. Monet accentuated this by failing to fit the whole façade on to his canvases, thus undercutting the notion of an architectural record and emphasizing his real subject – once again, the immense variety of colours and treatments of light to be found in the persistent study of a single subject.

Monet's final years were spent painting at his home, where he created an elaborate water-garden, an artificial organization of natural forms and of light and colour which best suited his pictorial aims. The majestic series of *Waterlily* studies occupied the last 20 years of his long life, and towards the end were painted with failing eyesight. Although more typical of the Japanese art he admired than of the Norman landscape, they cannot be ignored in our context. For many, the growing formlessness of the paintings, the subsuming of the subject into rich colour harmonies, seem almost completely abstract. Monet would have been horrified by this reaction to his work; the observation of nature as revealed by light and colour remained his ruling passion until the end.

By the beginning of the twentieth century the beaches of Normandy were very much in vogue as healthy weekend resorts for Parisians. It is no surprise, therefore, that we find such painters as Albert Marquet (1875–1947) and Georges Braque (1887–1963) working there in the kind of milieu described in Proust's novel *In Remembrance of Things Past*. Both were involved in the Fauve group of painters (see Mediterranean chapter). Marquet evolved a breezy and undemanding technique which suited well his taste for rather tawdry, commercialized seafronts with brash advertising hoardings and pleasure boats. His painterly technique was underpinned by considerable ability as a draughtsman. Braque also

GEORGES BRAQUE
HARBOUR IN NORMANDY, 1909
Art Institute, Chicago

Georges Braque, like Monet before him, had been raised on the coast of Normandy, and his affection for the area, with its picturesque harbours, bustling ports, passing tourists and peculiarly luminous cloudy skies never left him. His early enthusiasm for Fauve painting was largely dissipated after he met Picasso. By 1908 he was working out some of the innovations of Picasso's *Demoiselles d'Avignon* (1907), and was experimenting with the shallow spatial effects and tight formal structure of Cézanne's later work. What he added to both of these influences was greater abstraction from nature. In 1908, Braque exhibited a series of landscapes which he painted at L'Estaque on the Provençale coast, and these were the first paintings to earn the title Cubist. The following year he returned to Normandy, and continued the experiment. The style was, of course, anti-naturalistic and thus was in direct opposition to the work of the Impressionists and of Cézanne. Nevertheless, the assurance of Braque's compositions is not merely on a formal level, breaking down and reconstructing observed reality, but is of his brilliantly articulated and harmonized use of colour which seems to represent a natural progression from the dissolutions of form into orchestrations of colour found in the work of the later Impressionists.

CLAUDE MONET
FOUR POPLARS, 1891
Metropolitan Museum of Art, New York

was blessed with immense facility and although most noted as co-inventor, with Picasso, of Cubism, he was never doctrinaire and did not resist the temptation offered by a picturesque harbour.

In the work of both Braque and Marquet, eclectic painters who could exploit pictorial ideas from many quarters to their own ends, the viewer might be forgiven for looking back to the more instinctive work of Isabey, Jongkind and Boudin. The seashore subjects are much the same. What divides them, apart from a few decades, is the experience of Impressionism, for no longer are we looking at representations of specific landscape views but rather at paintings, pieces of canvas covered with pigment, which happen, almost accidentally, to take the landscape as a departure point.

When Impressionism was taken to its logical conclusion, as Monet had taken it, it became for younger painters not so much a reaffirmation of naturalism as an inspiration for abstraction. There is no doubt that Normandy can be described as the birthplace of Impressionism, but it was also the place where the first modern movement in art finally came to rest.

CLAUDE MONET
ROUEN CATHEDRAL, 1894
Musée d'Orsay, Paris

BRITTANY AND BISCAY

The southern part of France's long western coastline begins in Brittany and ends where the western Pyrenees meet the sea in the south-eastern corner of the Bay of Biscay. Both the vast Breton peninsula which thrusts out into the Atlantic, its northern coasts forming the southern end of the English Channel and its southern shores the northern edge of the Bay of Biscay, and the district of Gascony which forms much of the inner Biscay shoreline, retain a unique flavour and provincial remoteness all of their own.

The scenery of Brittany is enormously varied, lacking only in high mountains. Surrounded on three sides by sea, its jagged coastline runs for some 750 miles (1207 kilometres); rocky foreshores and cliffs, rising at points to over 300 feet (91 metres) as at Pointe du Raz, are broken by sheltered coves harbouring shellfish, seabirds and fishing villages. Occasionally the Atlantic rollers meet the land along broad, white beaches as at La Baule. The landscape, the people and the economy are dominated by the sea. It provides a means of living for all the coastal communities. Seaweed is used as fertilizer, and the windborne brine enriches the pastures. The warm currents of the North Atlantic Drift encourage the growth of palms and Mediterranean foliage and bring on early-ripening crops, such as strawberries; in less sheltered areas the frequent gales and storms which sweep in from the sea have denuded the landscape of all but the most tenacious lichens and coarse grasses.

Historically, Brittany has seen itself as apart from the rest of France. The native Bretons proved stubborn in the struggle to avoid Roman overlordship 2000 years ago, and later the region was never successfully incorporated into the Frankish domains.

The dukedom was not absorbed into the political structure of France until 1491 (its neighbouring inland buffer state of Anjou being annexed in 1481). By this time its population was relatively high (at over 40 persons per square kilometre), deriving its livelihood from fishing, shepherding, flax cultivation and the offshoot cottage industries of linen-making, wool-carding and spinning. Today the region's expertise in textile manufacture persists, and finds its most attractive expression in intricate lacemaking, each region having a distinctive style.

The inhabitants of the two provinces of Upper and Lower Brittany remain mainly rural: almost 70 per cent of a (now relatively low) population of just 3 million are still involved in fishing or farming. This harsh lifestyle is reflected, as so often in such communities, in a strongly-felt religious faith and a persistence of folk traditions and customs. This is especially true of Lower Brittany, where the Breton language is still occasionally spoken; indeed,

JAMES McNEILL WHISTLER
COAST OF BRITTANY, 1861
Wadsworth Atheneum, Hartford, Conn.

as recently as 1901 the clergy of Lower Brittany were forbidden to preach in Breton. Traditional costume, enriched with many varieties of local lace, is sometimes worn even today. The picturesque local architecture is unusual, the numerous churches dating back to the early Middle Ages having bastardized Romanesque and Norman features grafted on to older, more primitive local building styles.

During the sixteenth and seventeenth centuries Brittany shared a new prominence and wealth along with most of the north-western coastal areas of Europe. With the beginnings of overseas exploration and colonial exploitation, the North Atlantic and Channel ports found themselves at the apex of a new and increasingly wealthy worldwide trading network. The great ports of St Malo, Brest and Lorient, strategically placed at the southern entrance to the English Channel, rapidly became the premier French ports and the principal Atlantic bases for the rapidly growing French navy of Louis XIV. To the south, La Rochelle, Rochefort, Brouage and Bordeaux also gained from this prosperity and new prestige.

Although the economic importance of Brittany has declined (the same industries persist, but are less crucial in a modern economy), the region retained its strategic importance until the recent decline of European naval power. It is still, however, the principal base for France's long-range fishing fleets.

Below the Breton peninsula the long, flat coast of the Bay of Biscay runs almost due south, in a line broken only by the estuary of the river Garonne, to meet the western extremities of the Pyrenees and the Spanish border which marches with them. The hinterland of this sand-duned coast encompasses the regions of Médoc, the peculiar landscape of the Landes which has been reclaimed from the sea over the last three centuries, Guyenne and Gascony (another remote and semi-autonomous cultural district), all lying within an enormously vast expanse of heavily cultivated land at, or near, sea level.

Diaz de la Peña (1807–76) was born of Spanish parents at Bordeaux, the major city and port of the area. He is now remembered as a member of the Barbizon school (see South of Paris chapter), which he joined in the 1840s, but he also produced a number of large paintings and several oil sketches (much admired by Baudelaire) of the Landes region south of Bordeaux. Diaz painted in a manner influenced by Delacroix and by his training as a porcelain decorator (many of his earlier works are decorative Romantic studies of young rustic women set in rural glades). His rather turgid landscape style of heavy ground colours applied in thin washes, enlivened by rich primaries and a sparkling surface effect,

PAUL GAUGUIN
ROCKS BY THE SEA, 1886
Kunstmuseum, Gothenburg

wonderfully evoked the restless, windswept, raincast melancholy of the inner Biscay coast.

Brittany began to attract painters in the mid-nineteenth century. Daubigny painted some views of it and Eugène Boudin (1824–98) travelled there from his native Normandy (see Normandy chapter). Boudin's taste for seascapes and beach scenes led him naturally to this neighbouring coast. His great pupil Claude Monet (1840–1926), who was also raised in Normandy, often visited Brittany in the 1880s and 1890s. He was attracted by the dramatic rocky coast and turbulent seas of the southern shore of the peninsula. By this stage in his career Monet was immersed in his pursuit of a personal aesthetic: he had built his Japanese garden at his home in Giverny and was embarking on the extraordinary series of monumental treatments of recurring subjects – Rouen Cathedral, haystacks, early mornings on the Seine and the river Thames in twilight – which dominated his later work. The pictures produced in Brittany, especially at Belle Ile and around the Quiberon peninsula on the northern coast of Biscay, look forward to the later works in their persistent attempt to represent the same subject under subtly differing conditions. In the autumn of 1886 he produced some 40 canvases of the wild seashore of Belle Ile. However, they also seemed to mark an end to any desire to represent movement or action in his work. Monet's late works are static, all the painter's energy concentrated in capturing light and colour alone. In the violent seascapes painted in Brittany, Monet finally solved the problem of capturing the fleeting impression – the breaking wave, the flying spray, the glimpsed rock – and it no longer interested him.

Monet's friendship with James McNeill Whistler (1834–1903) appears to have prompted the latter to visit Brittany during the 1890s. He lived briefly in Paris from 1893–6, and at this late stage in his career was concentrating increasingly upon intimate, small-scale seascapes, landscapes and townscapes. Like the large *Nocturnes* of the 1870s, with which he established his notorious reputation as an aesthete *par excellence*, these remain carefully balanced 'arrangements' of colour and shape, rather than topographical views; however, they are informed by his facility as a neat graphic draughtsman (in the wake of a ruinous libel case against the

PAUL GAUGUIN
SNOW SCENE, 1888
Kuntsmuseum, Gothenburg

During Gauguin's first visits to Brittany (in 1886 and 1888) he painted a number of idyllic landscapes, some featuring local figures – shepherdesses, bathing boys – but mostly pure landscape. The motifs he selected in the latter views were similar to those favoured by the Impressionists, and his style at the time bore strong Impressionist characteristics especially in his use of dappled brushwork and a bright palette. However, when compared to the sort of paintings Monet was producing at the same time at Belle Ile, off the Breton coast, (see page 124), a sharp contrast is clear. Where the latter was struggling to capture the movement and violence of the elements, Gauguin's coast scenes (see page 115) were gentle and lyrical – closer in manner to a treatment of the same subject by Whistler (see page 113). It is apparent that Gauguin was gradually absorbing the quiet provincial atmosphere of the district, and adapting his style to convey something of this. It would not be long before a distinctly spiritual quality entered his vision of Brittany, the landscape, its inhabitants and their dwellings being subsumed into a strange mystical heaven on earth where everything has its place and order, the elements of this world bound together by a simple, visionary faith.

◀ PAUL GAUGUIN
THE VISION AFTER THE SERMON (JACOB WRESTLING WITH THE ANGEL), 1888
National Gallery of Scotland, Edinburgh

PAUL GAUGUIN
THE YELLOW HAYSTACKS, 1888
Musée d'Orsay, Paris

English critic Ruskin in 1877, which he won but was awarded damages of only a farthing, he rapidly regained a respectable income producing tourist views of Venice, then the most fashionable resort in Europe). These delicate studies preserve much of the atmosphere of the small Breton fishing villages which have now largely changed beyond recognition. It is interesting that Whistler's pupil, the English painter Walter Sickert (1860–1942) left a similarly evocative record of the seedier parts of Dieppe at the turn of the century.

Paul Signac (1863–1935) also found that the seashore provided him with certain formal values central to his style of painting. A close follower of the rather serious Neo-Impressionist Seurat (see Rivers chapter), he soon rejected the radical social and political concerns of his mentor while following and developing his pictorial style in a more decorative manner. A keen yachtsman, the greater part of his work was completed while navigating both the Atlantic and Mediterranean coasts of France (see Mediterranean chapter). Although he consistently developed the systematized *pointilliste* technique of Divisionism established by Seurat (where the painted image is made up of thousands of individual dabs of pure colour of more or less equal, minuscule size), the compositional rigour of Seurat's initial influence soon gave way to an increasingly picturesque quality. Indeed, in Signac's later canvases the choice of colour moves away from carefully observed tones towards more emotive and romantic colours. Signac's work in Brittany – probably because of the more rugged coastline and rough seas which characterize the area – is rather more violent in subject than the usually placid and lifeless compositions associated with Neo-Impressionism/Divisionism. One may safely ascribe this to his enthusiasm for sailing, although his chosen style was probably the least suited for conveying the vigour and activity of a life on the waves.

All these painters found in the landscape, or seashore, of Brittany suitable subjects for their canvases. Only Monet seems to have been drawn there for a very specific reason – the violent breakers of the Quiberon peninsula. However, at the same time a separate group of artists became fascinated not only by the land- and seascapes of the area, but by the strangely distinctive local atmosphere, character and inhabitants.

François Bonvin (1817–87), the Realist painter and follower of Courbet whose work was influenced by seventeenth-century Dutch and French genre paintings, had exhibited several picturesque Breton peasant scenes in the salons of the 1860s and enjoyed some modest success. Then, in 1862, two friends of the landscape painter Corot, Français and Anastasi, 'discovered' the

PAUL GAUGUIN
LE POULDU, 1890
National Gallery of Art, Washington DC

village of Pont-Aven and the nearby harbour of Le Pouldu, on the southern face of the Breton peninsula between the ports of Lorient and Quimper. By the 1870s a steady stream of painters from all over Europe were visiting the village, staying at either the Pension Gloanec or at the Villa Julia. With the arrival of Paul Gauguin in June 1886 the locality took on a new importance as the centre of a group of artists stimulated not only by Gauguin and by each other but also by the potential of a specific, limited region within which they could work out their ideas.

For Gauguin, Brittany represented only a step in a journey away from convention and urban civilization, a journey which began with his resignation from the stock exchange in 1883 and which would end in disease and obscurity 7000 miles away in Polynesia. He had just walked out on his wife and family, and his Parisian landlord advised him that Madame Gloanec at Pont-Aven was prepared to extend long-term credit. Attracted by the opportunity to avoid the mundane tribulations of everyday existence with which he was singularly ill-equipped to deal, Gauguin set off for Brittany. Here he found two things which immediately appealed to him. Firstly, an atmosphere of timeless, simple continuity which stemmed from a culture proud of and bound up with its past; the bonds were those of folk tradition, native language and an unquestioned religious faith. Secondly, he came upon a group of young painters who had already perceived these qualities, but who in their inexperience had failed to find an adequate means to reflect their enthusiasm in their work.

Gauguin's reputation hitherto was based on a style of Impressionist painting derived from that of Pissarro but showing less naturalistic control and a more restless urge for expression through shapes and bright, contrasting colours. He was increasingly dissatisfied by the naturalistic limitations of Impressionism, felt 'shackled by the need of probability', and yearned for 'the translation of thought into a medium other than literature'; his ambitions in this direction were high and exacting, wishing to capture in form and paint 'phenomena which appear to us as supernatural' – nothing less than the mythical and spiritual inner life of mankind.

During Gauguin's first visit he merely absorbed the atmosphere, sketching and painting straightforward landscapes and still lifes. He does not appear to have been popular among the more conventional painters visiting the district. He would hold court in the Pension Gloanec, giving impromptu and tedious lectures on art. He called the mistress of another painter a 'slop bucket'. He was described as making 'drawings of geese', and he dressed, according to the Scottish painter A.S. Hartrick, 'like a Breton fisherman in a blue jersey and wore a beret jauntily on the side of his head . . . In manner he was self-contained and confident, silent and almost dour, though he could unbend and be quite charming when he liked.'

For Gauguin, Brittany represented a new world: 'I love Brittany. I find wildness and primitiveness there. When my wooden shoes ring on this granite I hear the muffled, dull and powerful tone which I try to achieve in painting.' Nevertheless, the winter climate did not agree with him, and he travelled to Martinique and Panama in 1887.

Gauguin returned to Brittany in 1888, and began painting in a manner which reflected a variety of disparate influences: the strong contours of Japanese prints, the patterns of Caribbean and Breton folk art, the formal solidity of Italian quattrocento painting and the simple stone sculptures adorning Breton churches.

During his previous visit Gauguin had met a young painter named Emile Bernard (1868–1941). The meeting was not a success. Now they met again, and a productive relationship began. Bernard had been painting in a manner presenting flat colours within heavy contours or outlines which he and Louis Anquetin called 'cloisonné' after the style of enamel inlay. For Bernard, painting was an essentially decorative pursuit; for Gauguin the conjunction of his own ideas with Bernard's formal patterning produced *The Vision after the Sermon – Jacob Wrestling* (1888), his first successful synthesis in paint of outer and inner life. Breton peasant women, their black costumes and white headdresses making them nun-like, strike devotional postures; before them, and separated from them by a tree, struggle Jacob and the Angel in an unmodulated landscape.

From this achievement developed a unique body of work – referred to as that of a school, but really simply a group of like-minded painters, including Armand Séguin, Charles Filiger, Maurice Maufra and the Dutchman Meyer de Haan. Their styles and subjects were all similar, their work was geographically concentrated around Pont-Aven and Le Pouldu, their motivation devolved from Gauguin and, to a lesser degree, Bernard. The latter was to claim, in later life, a large slice of the credit for developing the Pont-Aven manner; this was partly true, but he, like the others, was not as able as Gauguin to transcend his sources. Their paintings remain, on the whole, unusually stylized representations of peasant life and the village landscape, often having little more than a celebratory, nostalgic feeling and a hint of condescension towards their subjects. The work of the Pont-Aven group nevertheless helped to break down many barriers in the selection and representation of everyday life and landscape. Their use of broad areas of non-naturalistic colour and strangely simplified forms looked forward to the experiments in abstraction at the beginning of the twentieth century.

The most promising and gifted painter to visit Gauguin and the Pont-Aven circle was Paul Sérusier (1863–1927), who stayed at the Pension Gloanec in the summer of 1888; he mixed with the more traditional, academic painters, but became curious about the work and techniques of Gauguin's circle. This was probably unavoidable, for although Gauguin himself was living in a rented house just outside Pont-Aven, the group's work was hung in the Pension (causing one enraged *paysagiste* to threaten to walk out if any more of Gauguin's works were hung). Bernard effected an introduction, and Sérusier spent a morning painting under Gauguin's supervision. The result, which altered the young painter's life, was *The Talisman*, one of the key works in the development of abstract art, painted on the lid of a cigar box.

Upon his return to Paris Sérusier promoted the work and the ideas it represented, which had a decisive influence on Maurice Denis, Edouard Vuillard, Pierre Bonnard, and others of the group known as the Nabis (see Paris chapter). Denis described the genesis of the painting, the birth of the style known as *Synthétisme*:

> Sérusier revealed Gauguin's name to us, and showed us, not without some mystery, the cover of a cigar box upon which one could make out a

PAUL SÉRUSIER
THE TALISMAN, 1888
Musée d'Orsay, Paris

EMILE BERNARD
PONT AVEN, c.1888
Museo Albi

shapeless landscape, synthetically formulated in violet, vermilion, Veronese green, and other pure colours, just as they came from the tube, and almost unmixed with white. 'How do you see that tree?' Gauguin had asked in the Bois d'Amour. 'Is it green? Then put on green, the finest green on your palette; – and that shadow, is it a bit blue? Don't be afraid to paint it as blue as possible.'

Another strand of influence, this time stretching further afield – to Provence – came about when Gauguin visited Van Gogh in Arles in October 1888. He took with him a painting by Bernard, which Van Gogh copied; thereafter strong linear contours bound the coloured areas and planes in his work, although the colours within these contours remain more vividly worked up and patterned than any produced by the Pont-Aven group. (See Provence chapter.)

In 1889 Volpini, the proprietor of the Café des Arts in Paris, put on the first public exhibition of the work of the Pont-Aven group under the title *'Groupe Impressioniste et Synthétiste'*. There was little public response, and that was largely unfavourable. Gaugin was by now disillusioned and broke. In 1891 he left for Tahiti, although he returned to France briefly in 1893–95. His most significant acquisition while in Brittany during that period was a broken ankle gained in a brawl in a sailors' bar in Concarneau. Nevertheless, his final visit set the seal on the popularity of Brittany as not only a region of immense appeal for landscape painters but also as a centre for the disaffected and the avant-garde.

Among the many notable figures who worked there at about the same time were Charles Cottet, Roderic O'Conor and Alfred Stevens. Cottet was based at Camaret, near Ouessant. He too responded to the unique

combination of peasant life and the strange maritime landscape, living among the fishermen all his working life and producing gentle, melancholy paintings. His work was known to the Pont-Aven school. The Irish painter Roderic O'Conor, one of Gauguin's close friends, produced strong landscapes in pure colours which were much admired by the Bloomsbury circle in England, while Alfred Stevens, the leading English painter, set something of a fashion for the peninsula among British artists. It is interesting, in this context, to find that the leading English modern landscapist John Piper, noted for his proto-Romantic treatments of classical architecture and ruins, produced a series of mature abstract landscapes in Brittany in the 1960s which look back to his early, purely abstract works of the early 1930s. In these works the timeless function of the Breton landscape as a subject for painters has gone full circle; it is the varying light and atmosphere, the movement and interplay of water and seashore which again absorb the artist's attention.

CLAUDE MONET
ROUGH SEA AT BELLE ILE,
1886
Louvre, Paris

JOHN PIPER
THE COAST OF BRITTANY I,
1961
Tate Gallery, London

The coast of Brittany has provoked many and varied reactions among painters, and provides a fine example of how the artistic temperament selects only what it needs from any given subject. The various reactions to it by Whistler and Gauguin have been discussed (see page 117). One of the most notable painters of Brittany outside the Pont-Aven school was Monet. His lack of any interest in the inhabitants of the area makes the content and style of his pictures very different from that of Gauguin and his followers; for him Belle Ile, off the southern coast of the Breton peninsula, was a location in which he could study the elements in the raw, the swirling seas battering the rocky cliffs, clouds of spray and brine forced up into the turbulent skies above the coast. The pictures Monet painted here are among his most dramatic, dealing as much with movement and force as with light and colour. For the English Romantic and sometime abstract painter, John Piper, the colours and textures of the Breton coast (so sharply captured by Monet) provided a starting point for a series of charming, informal works in which natural forms and sensations are played off against the hard-edged shapes so favoured by English abstract painters.

PROVENCE

PAUL CÉZANNE
LANDSCAPE WITH ROCKS AND TREES, 1895
Kunsthaus, Zürich

The mountainous region of Provence lies at the south-west corner of the French landmass between the lower reaches of the river Rhône to the west and the Italian border to the east. The upland block at the core of the region represents the eastern foothills of the southerly tail of the Alps, which swing up from the Mediterranean coast, following the French border towards Switzerland before curving east towards Austria and the northern marches of Yugoslavia. This great volcanic arc of landmass forms one of Europe's outstanding natural features and is the principal barrier between Italy and the rest of northern Europe.

Provence shares many characteristics with the other mountain regions of France examined in the Mountains chapter. It is remote from the capital, Paris, and lies as far from the traditional seat of political power in the Ile de France as do the Pyrenees. As in the other mountainous regions, its inhabitants, apart from those living along the Mediterranean coast, derive the greater part of their living from the land. However, Provence supports a larger population than one might expect given its hilly terrain. This is because Provence is more agriculturally sophisticated than comparable regions elsewhere in France. The usual upland farming activity of livestock rearing is widespread, but is practised on a more or less equal balance with cultivation, the development of which has as much to do with the favourable climate as with the slightly less rugged terrain than that of, say, the Jura or the Massif Central. Both plateaux and valley floor are, where possible, brought under the plough; the crops raised range from hard wheats and maize to early market garden crops such as pimentos and soft fruits, and even some sub-tropical species such as aubergines. The lower slopes are often terraced to support orchards, olive and orange groves and, on south-facing slopes, grape vines – the dry red wines of Provence, such as Châteauneuf-du-Pape, are widely celebrated. This agricultural diversification means that Provence has always been substantially richer than the other upland areas of France.

The potential of the favourable climate is reflected in the natural topography and vegetation. The area is irrigated by streams and rivers fed all year round by the ice caps of the Maritime Alps. The range of altitude encompassed in the region of Provence, from high Alp to sea level, is matched by a broad spectrum of natural vegetation, from coniferous woods in the upper climes, broadleaf deciduous trees and shrubs in the temperature altitudes and valleys, to typically Mediterranean vegetation of scrub, spiky grasses, olive and cypress trees and agave near sea level.

Like other mountain areas Provence retains a strong sense of regional distinction, preserved in folklore and in

the Provençal dialect (once spoken throughout the Midi) which still survives in certain pockets today. There is a unique feeling of cultural and historical continuity engendered among the local people and, as in Brittany, the spine of this continuity is provided by the church.

Historically, agriculture was not the sole source of Provençal prosperity, for its location at the southwestern edge of the Alps meant that the region was a pivotal point in trade and communications between Italy and the eastern Mediterranean and the lands north and west of the Alps. As long ago as the fourth century BC, Greek trading colonies were established around the mouth of the Rhône for the specific purpose of fostering a lucrative interchange of goods with the Celtic peoples of France and Germany – colonies that were later taken over by the Romans in the first century BC.

The name Provence derives from the Latin *Provincia Gallia*, a shorthand term for the group of Roman provinces in France (Provence, with the rest of the Mediterranean coast and a hinterland stretching north to Lyons, was correctly termed Gallia Narbonensis). However, Provence was the first Gallic region a Roman traveller entered as he moved west of the Alpine barrier, so the nickname stuck. The major Roman towns of

PAUL CÉZANNE
MONT STE VICTOIRE,
1904–6
Philadelphia Museum of Art

Mont Ste Victoire was for Cézanne the principal landscape motif for the last twenty years of his life, and it was in this momentous struggle with the mountain that Cézanne came closest to realizing his artistic aims and aspirations. In the first paintings of the subject, dating from the mid-1880s many details of the landscape persist in crowding out the main motif– framing devices such as trees, foreground details and buildings. By the turn of the century these had been eliminated, and this vast rocky bluff (which Cézanne's studio confronted) had become a cypher, a cult image in which any original meanings and associations had been erased, to make way for an elaborate patterning of colour, whether in oil (above) or watercolour (opposite), in which the paint begins to lose its representational function in favour of the central life – the 'soul' – of the picture itself.

Massilia (Marseilles) and Aquae Sextiae (Aix-en-Provence) were linked to Rome by the Via Aurelia, which followed the Ligurian coast and was one of the first international highways in western Europe. Massilia was also linked to the heart of the Roman empire by sea, and became the major entrepôt for the Gallic provinces. Provence is littered with substantial Roman remains, especially along the lower reaches of the river Rhône – for example, the vast amphitheatres at Orange and Arles, a triumphal arch at Carpentras, a complete Roman town at Vaison-la-Romaine, and other features at St Remy and Avignon.

During the Middle Ages commerce up the Rhône increased, and Arles (originally a Celtic foundation) became the capital of a small kingdom, later a republic, and an influential archbishopric. Avignon, to the north, became the seat of a much more significant religious power in 1305 when Pope Clement V took up formal residence there, under French protection, to avoid the violent rivalry and conflicts which shook the papacy and see of Rome during the thirteenth and fourteenth centuries. The massive papal palace in Avignon and the small state associated with it remained in use until 1417, although an alternative Pope, proclaimed in Rome in 1378, eventually wrested power from the papacy in Avignon. This period of schism made Provence a focal point of the medieval political scene, and the region remains rich in churches, monasteries and castles. It was also the home of the medieval minstrel poets or troubadours who travelled the local courts and seigneurial seats, and the great Italian medieval poet Petrarch lived for four years at Fontaine de Vaucluse near Avignon.

Provence was annexed to the centralized French state in 1481, and thereafter the strategically important coastal ports and commercially important riverine settlements were fortified and economically bolstered as the principal springboards for French power projection in the Mediterranean. However, there was little here to attract industry apart from the existence of some natural minerals, and the Provençal bluffs resisted the incursions of later economic development and modern lines of communication; even today only one railway line crosses the region, running diagonally along the valley of the Durance from Aix to Sisteron and then north to Gap, while a single motorway has been built across the difficult terrain between Aix and Cannes. The landscape has thus remained remarkably unaltered – a historical landscape rather than a wild one, and one which has not been denuded or destroyed by the inroads of modern progress. In this it is unique; the more disruptive techniques of modern agriculture have not really taken root here and the area has remained almost untouched by warfare, apart from a brief and unsuccessful attempt at invasion by Mussolini in June 1940, when Italian divisions were stopped in their tracks by French troops. In recent years a series of major forest fires has substantially damaged the vegetation cover, although the climate and reafforestation programmes have conspired to restore this as quickly as possible.

PAUL CÉZANNE
MONT STE VICTOIRE, 1906
Tate Gallery, London

This, then, is the rich setting for the outstanding paintings of two of the most influential and popular artists of the last 100 years: Paul Cézanne (1839–1906) and Vincent Van Gogh (1853–1890). The former lived near Aix-en Provence for most of his mature working life, from 1887 until his death; Van Gogh was in Provence for only two short years prior to his suicide in 1890, a period which was dominated by intermittent bouts of insanity and yet was surprisingly fruitful. Their work in Provence is not comparable, and indeed the two had little to do with one another, but both painters produced images of a landscape which remain the most familar views of France ever painted outside Paris.

Paul Cézanne was born in Aix-en-Provence, the son of a well-to-do banker. One of his firmest friends at school was Emile Zola, who later introduced him to Manet and Courbet and encouraged him to abandon the study of law and move to Paris in 1861 to become a painter. Cézanne's paintings in the 1860s represent a strange attempt to define a style through a shocking Romanticism. Often erotic and over-dramatic, and probably influenced by the sensationalism of Zola's writing, these pictures (such as *The Rape*, 1867) were not well received,

◀ VINCENT VAN GOGH
WHEATFIELDS AT LA CRAU, NEAR ARLES, 1888
Vincent Van Gogh Museum, Amsterdam

VINCENT VAN GOGH
THE CAFÉ AT NIGHT, 1888
Rijksmuseum Kröller-Müller, Otterlo

but they reveal an impetuousness combined with a painterly tendency which steadily grew over the length of Cézanne's career.

Another acquaintance Cézanne made during the 1860s was Camille Pissarro, and when the latter moved to Auvers-sur-Oise, near Pontoise, in 1872, Cézanne joined him and began to paint pure landscape (see North of Paris chapter). His work with Pissarro was a turning point; he learnt the value of working from nature and of an analytical approach to both colour and brushwork. Cézanne exhibited with the Impressionists in 1874 and 1877, but he never fully agreed with their aims. He consistently seemed to be more interested in a structural reappraisal of the natural scene before him – whether landscape, still life or portrait – than with the passing impression of movement, light and colour. A second turning point in his career came with the death of his father in 1886.

Cézanne had spent two largely unhappy decades in and around Paris, interspersed with long periods painting in Provence. During the Franco-Prussian war he had gone there to escape conscription, eventually staying at L'Estaque on the Provençal coast. In 1878, following critical failure at the 1877 Impressionist exhibition, he retreated to the family home at Jas de Bouffon outside Aix, this time bringing his mistress Hortense Fiquet, of whom his father did not approve, and their son. The year 1880 once again found him at L'Estaque, and during this period Cézanne seems to have acquired some confidence in his style (see Mediterranean chapter). In 1882 he had a picture accepted at the Salon. However, in 1886 he inherited the family estate, leaving him with a reasonable income and a home; he finally married Hortense Fiquet and moved back to Aix, where he spent most of the rest of his life (although he still indulged in working trips to Paris, and could afford to rent houses in various places whenever he wished). It seems that the limiting influence on him of an unsatisfactory relationship with his father and the frustration over his lack of success in the Parisian art world had now come to an end. So, too, had his

friendship with Zola. In 1886 his old friend published the novel *L'Oeuvre*, in which the central character, a painter, is presented as an unsuccessful man driven as much by frustration as by the selfish and single-minded pursuit of a nebulous vision. Cézanne saw much of himself in Zola's creation and took umbrage, effectively severing relations with his valued friend and, for the most part, with the rest of the artistic establishment.

For the last 20 years of his life Cézanne withdrew into social and cultural seclusion, gaining a reputation of being difficult and unapproachable. With hindsight we can see that this withdrawal from the world at large was a central element in his art; between 1880 and his death Cézanne produced some 1300 paintings which reflect a long, contemplative and painful quest for a grail which was inevitably unattainable. However, the paintings which chart this quest tell a story of outstanding working consistency and great creative development.

The most constant preoccupation of these mature years was the landscape of Provence, which offered Cézanne both the greatest scope for stylistic development and his greatest challenge. The still lifes of this period allowed him to carefully organize and balance the composition before him; because of this they remain in many ways Cézanne's most satisfying works. At the other extreme, his portraits and figure studies appear to have provided his greatest source of frustration; he abandoned his portrait of the art dealer Ambroise Vollard after over 100 sittings, declaring that he was barely satisfied with the shirt! His prolific landscape works, in oil and watercolour, sit between these two extremes. Cézanne exercised compositional control by returning again and again to a handful of local views – the coastal port of L'Estaque (see Mediterranean chapter), the rocky outcrops around Aix, the nearby quarry of Bibemus, and his favourite motif, Mont Ste Victoire.

The process of Cézanne's rejection of Impressionism was underpinned by a growing sense of solidity and formal structure in his painting. His work displays increasingly ambitious attempts to convey, through choice of colour, refinement of shape and the undisguised methods of applying paint itself, a wide range of seemingly disconnected temperamental responses to his subject. That is not to say that his work by the 1880s was disorganized or undisciplined – quite the contrary – but that his aim was never clearly focused. Like Turner, he was ill-equipped to define his purpose in any other manner than through constant experimentation and adaptation of his working method. There are a handful of oft-quoted hints as to his major concerns: he had a desire

VINCENT VAN GOGH
LES ALYCAMPS, ARLES, 1888
Rijksmuseum Kröller-Müller, Otterlo

Among the most objective, charming and controlled landscapes Van Gogh produced during his time in Provence were views of the parks, gardens and esplanades of the provincial towns there. In this wonderful example, reminiscent of the decorative finesse of the Nabis painters of Paris such as Vuillard (see page 42), Van Gogh's sheer virtuosity as a painter is clear, untroubled by the tortured self-expression which characterizes so much of his work. The diagonal composition was a favourite of Van Gogh's, and the thrusting elision of the perspective (as though we have been placed closer to the scene than intended) was a technique learned from Van Gogh's intense study of Japanese prints. So, too, was the drawing of form in solid outlines and contours, filling in the volumes with areas of nearly flat colour. The assurance of the composition and of the style, most clearly shown in the confidence of his colours and the almost epigrammatic draughtsmanship, give only a taste of the immense potential the Dutchman had, before he cut his life short by committing suicide.

P. Gauguin. 88

PAUL GAUGUIN
LES ALYCAMPS, ARLES, 1888
Musée d'Orsay, Paris

to 'make of Impressionism something solid and durable, like the art of the museums'; he sought to 'do Poussin again, from nature'. But these pronouncements can be misleading, and tell us less about Cezanne's art than the paintings themselves.

There is a formal structure, which can be associated with classicism, in Cézanne's work, the sort of structure often rejected or ignored by the Impressionists. It is imposed by the careful control of brushwork, often used to establish a pattern on the canvas which exposes the synthetic nature of the painting before us – it is not meant to be an accurate representation of the landscape or object in front of the artist, but rather is clearly his reconstruction of it. Other structural features employed by Cézanne to embellish this effect were pronounced outlines or contours (not often used by the strict Impressionists), a warping or distortion of traditional perspective in order to satisfy the pictorial design, and a harmonized sculpting in colour – again, the choice of colours is not meant to be naturalistic but obviously synthetic. These elements in Cézanne's style combine to set him apart from Impressionism; on the other hand, his emphasis on colour as opposed to accurate draughtsmanship sets him apart from the classical tradition. Both features mark in his work something unique and quite innovative. Further, we are made aware in a way which is rare in the history of art – the work of Rembrandt and Goya being notable exceptions – of the painful effort the artist has expended in achieving his final image, and in this Cézanne prefigures the egoism of much twentieth-century art.

These aspects of his work, however, do not devalue the intense feeling for nature and for the landscape of Provence which is communicated in Cézanne's paintings. The lucid colours of the southern atmosphere were a perfect foil for his palette, already lightened and made more vivacious during his period with Pissarro at Auvers-sur-Oise; the delicate tonal variations of blues and greens set against pale oranges and delicate red-browns – the range which dominated Cézanne's palette – wonderfully evoke the feel of Provence.

Cézanne worked across the canvas as a whole, pushing the same mix of paint carried on the brush into disparate areas of the image, which helped to build up a concerted, harmonious result. Often foreground details are muted to effervescent pinks and blue-greens which reappear on the horizon or in the sky itself. He usually adopted a high viewpoint, to which the upland topography of Provence lent itself, reducing the area occupied by sky so that the canvas was filled with the patterning parallel brushwork with which he reconstructed the details of the landscape.

The Provence revealed to us in Cézanne's work is not a commercial landscape, nor a conspicuously historical one, but rather a series of extensive views of dramatic features (usually mountains), framed by foreground trees (usually the knotty pines of the middle slopes) with villages or houses set in the foreground (usually viewed from above, showing little more than the slanting roofs and chimneys). There are some paintings and colour sketches of wooded glades, with rocks, which allowed Cézanne to darken his palette and play with more intense contrasts of light and shade. These are often indistinguishable from paintings produced during his working visits to the Ile de France of the same period.

We can see from this brief survey that the features which interested Cézanne were formal; he was not concerned with selecting a picturesque view or with the lives of the inhabitants, but rather with a natural arrangement of shapes and colours which lent themselves to his pictorial experimentation. People are completely absent from these landscapes, as is evidence of any activity, such as farming or fishing. The paintings remain attempts to create, through the use of colour, a sense of enduring formal unity and cohesion. This grand aim is his strongest link with Poussin, although there is also a series of ambitious paintings combining landscape with nude figures which also look back, this time in subject as well as style, via Manet's *Déjeuner sur l'Herbe* to Poussin (and which also look forward to the work of Matisse and other classically-informed painters of the twentieth century – see Mediterranean chapter). In the sequence of *Bathers* paintings Cézanne reduced the arrangement of human forms to almost geometric abstractions, detail and draughtsmanship sacrificed on the altar of formal harmony. This is also true of their setting; in *Les Grandes Baigneuses* (1898–1905) anatomical details – heads and limbs – are actually missing from the sculptural figures, which are organized in two tightly constructed knots which interrelate with the curiously arched tree trunks in the middle ground. These paintings represent Cézanne's most extreme attempt to resolve the classical tradition with the Impressionism at the root of his art. The landscape here is no more realistic than those of Poussin.

By the turn of the century Cézanne's gradual development had reached a point which verged on abstraction. In the final series of paintings of Mont Ste Victoire (of which there are many in both oil and watercolour, Cézanne having built a studio confronting the mountain which dominates the landscape around Aix), details of the landscape became unimportant – it is often impossible to tell whether a patch of colour represents a house or a tree – and the ephemeral effects of wind or fleeting sunshine are ignored, while the thrust towards total harmony remains intact. Many of these works appear unfinished – although the notion of finish meant nothing to Cézanne; the painter referred to 'realizing' the painted image, a continuing process and one which meant – given his technique of working across the canvas with equal emphasis – that at any given stopping point the painting would hold together.

In the late oil paintings Cézanne's choice of colours became darker, the better to increase the range of hues and tones available to him. In these monumental canvases we can see how Cézanne's work prefigures some of the abstract painters of the twentieth century, especially the Cubists and de Staël (see Mediterranean chapter).

With the exception of the *Bathers* paintings, Cézanne worked directly from nature, painting landscapes, either from his studio or *en plein air*. On 15 October 1906 he was caught in a torrential thunderstorm and subsequently developed pneumonia, from which he died a week later.

Only during the last five years of his life had Cézanne begun to receive the critical acclaim which had eluded him for so long. Vincent Van Gogh did not live long enough to enjoy even such belated success. His work in Provence presents a very different view of the region from that of Cézanne and at the same time tells us more about the state of mind of the painter.

He was born the son of a Protestant minister, in the small Dutch village of Groot-Zundert, and worked for a firm of art dealers from 1869–75. He then attempted to pursue a religious career, working as a lay preacher in the Belgian mining region of Borinage. There his extreme self-sacrifice endangered his life and, having been relieved, he spent some months as a tramp. In 1881 he decided to become an artist and, during the remaining ten years of his life, produced over 800 paintings and a similar number of drawings. He was an impatient student and swiftly chose to reject any academic discipline in favour of Realism, concentrating on the plight of the agricultural peasantry. He copied the works of Millet, but worked in a heavy, dark, impasto style. From this time on he subsisted on advances from his younger brother Theo, and it is from his numerous and detailed letters to Theo that we derive much of our biographical knowledge of his later life.

In 1886 Van Gogh went to Paris, where the impact of Impressionism and of the Japanese prints then in fashion transformed both his style and his subject matter. He realised that the powerful emotional effect he was seeking could be achieved most successfully by using expressive colours, shapes and compositional forms. The Impressionists may have unveiled to him the potential of bright colours, but he had no concern for their naturalism. He wrote: 'Instead of trying to reproduce exactly what I have before my eyes, I use colour more arbitrarily so as to express myself more forcibly.'

He adopted a style similar to that of the Divisionist painters which allowed him to apply pure colour in small dabs to the canvas, often in adjacent contrast, creating a vibrant effect. His paintings in Paris show the rapid development of a cohesive and considerably assured style of painting, his primary subject matter now being landscapes and views of the city suburbs. Eventually Van Gogh found the hubbub and frivolity of Paris too disrupting an influence and he settled at Arles in February 1888, the beginning of an intensely prolific period (he painted over 200 canvases in his first 15 months in Provence). Van Gogh admired the compositional invention and bright colours of Japanese prints, which he collected and which sometimes appear in his portraits, but they also represented a vision of an ideal, simple society living in harmony with nature. Provence seemed to offer similar possibilities: 'Here my life will become more and more like a Japanese painter's, living close to nature. . . .' In the train going to Provence, he peered out to see 'if it was Japan yet', and the first few weeks in Arles seemed to satisfy his hopes: 'This country seems to me as beautiful as Japan as far as the limpidity of the atmosphere and the gay colour effects are concerned.'

During his first months in Provence Van Gogh worked with positive gusto and enthusiasm, despite his terrible poverty (he sold none of his pictures), undernourishment and acute addiction to tobacco and alcohol. A series of views of local parks, seascapes with the distinctive Provençal fishing boats and a series of still lifes centred around his lodgings (including his first *Sunflower* pictures) all show a refreshingly simple and direct relation with the natural world about him; he began to use very bright colours which were applied now in more flowing and rhythmical brushstrokes and unusual compositional designs (derived from his Japanese influences). Most of the paintings of this period are positive and delightful records of Van Gogh's revelation of a kind of earthly paradise and of the impact of the southern sunlight on his northern mentality. This is especially true of the harvest scenes around Arles, painted in the late summer. His social conscience still found an outlet in the inclusion of farmers and fishermen, but any overt social message was not emphasized. Van Gogh's feeling for the human condition was reserved for the remarkable series of portraits of acquaintances which began during this period.

However, he suffered periodic bouts of depression and had began to doubt his sanity. In his letters references to the low life of brothels and bars jostle with joyous

VINCENT VAN GOGH
COUNTRY ROAD BY NIGHT, 1890
Rijksmuseum Kröller-Müller, Otterlo

ANDRÉ DUNOYER DE SEGONZAC
THE ROAD FROM GRIMAUD, 1937
Tate Gallery, London

descriptions of his new-found freedom. He seemed to be leading a double life. Among the works of this period can be found some disturbing evidence of his state of mind. *The Night Café* (1888) is an infernal vision, the interior of one of his haunts in Arles described in unsettlingly sharp perspective and intense reds, greens and yellows and populated by isolated, hunched figures. Van Gogh wrote of the painting: 'I have tried to express the idea that the café is a place where one can ruin oneself, go mad or commit a crime.' The brushwork and the diagonal recession are vertiginous; we read the painting as a kind of danger sign. The same can be said of its sister work,

Café at Night (1888), where the nocturnal street is imbued with a threatening luminosity which emanates both from the artificial light of the café and from the strange treatment of the night sky.

Van Gogh dreamt of establishing a sort of artistic commune in the sun and warmth of the south, and in May 1888 Theo forwarded him enough money to purchase a small house in Arles. He invited his friend Gauguin to stay and he arrived towards the end of the year. Gauguin soon realized something was wrong; Van Gogh was frequently hallucinating, probably from lack of food, and appeared to have been eating his pigments. His friend attempted to draw the Dutchman away from his intense, and by now obsessive, observation of nature by encouraging him to work more from the imagination. Violent quarrels between the two painters ended in Van Gogh's vicious (and unsuccessful) assault on Gauguin, an episode which culminated in his severing part of his own ear. Gauguin returned to Paris on Christmas Eve.

This event upset Van Gogh even more than Gauguin, for he realized how close to the edge of sanity he had come. He became terrified of being alone, and in May 1889 he voluntarily entered an asylum at St Remy. Here he once again worked frantically, in his lucid moments, producing over 150 paintings, most of them landscapes. His style increasingly reflected his inner turmoil; the canvases, although containing less shocking contrasts of colour than before, became frenzied whirlpools of brushwork. The compositions are often strung around the alarming diagonal perspective used in *The Night Café*. The elements of the landscape are consciously selected and simplified and become an anchor with reality as the style in which they are painted slips further away from naturalism towards delirium. Figures reminiscent of those of Millet reappear in his work – perhaps another attempt to relate to the normal world – but they are often so isolated and bowed beneath invisible burdens that they seem close in spirit to Van Gogh's fellow inmates. Nevertheless, the concentrated intensity of the landscapes painted through 1889 and at the beginning of 1890 represents a remarkable achievement; it is as though Van Gogh, perceiving an impending doom and struggling with his illness, sought to set down as much of himself in paint as possible. The landscape of Provence, seen through his eyes, can never be forgotten; but it has also become part of our image of Van Gogh's interior, mental landscape.

In May 1890 he felt sufficiently stable to travel north, visiting Theo in Paris then settling at Auvers-sur-Oise under the protective wing of the dilettante collector Dr Paul Gachet. Another period of intense work filled the remaining weeks of his life (see North of Paris chapter).

For all the beauty and popularity of the paintings of Provence by Van Gogh and Cézanne, they remain underpinned by a sense of frustration and struggle, and, for the former, by tragedy. A more balanced record of the Provençal landscape was provided by the painter and engraver André Dunoyer de Segonzac (1884–1974). He was at the forefront of a movement of naturalistic artists which grew up following the First World War (during which he was a camouflage designer). He worked in most genres and media, in a style initially influenced by the expressionism of Van Gogh but considerably muted and controlled. During the 1920s he also absorbed much of the compositional balance and rhythmic brushwork of Cézanne. In watercolour his style was looser, and he produced a large body of landscapes in this medium, many of them set in Provence. His prolific work as an etcher is belied in watercolour by his use of colour washes laid over linear details which have been drawn in pen and ink. His palette shows the limited tonalities associated with Cézanne and with the Cubists, built around orchestrations of greens and browns. Thus his representation of Provence was not as dynamic or vivid as that of his two great forebears, but he captured the feeling of a timeless agricultural pocket of land more successfully than either of them. We can feel here a landscape which exists outside the twentieth century; de Segonzac was very conscious of the French tradition stretching back, via Courbet, to Corot, and his eclectic watercolour style often echoes the expressiveness of the English Grand Tourists of the eighteenth century. This is fitting, as his work was primarily Romantic in motivation. The Provençal features which appealed to his eye were those which evidenced a traditional way of life – country lanes, harvest fields dotted with stooked corn, the old, slightly unkempt orchards and groves of the lower hillsides.

Thus we can see three distinct approaches to the painting of Provence, approaches not linked merely geographically but intertwined at various levels stylistically and thematically. For Cézanne, the countryside was a series of dramatic forms which he nevertheless treated as passive objects, springboards for an intense dialogue between the artist and his means of expression. For Van Gogh it was alternately a source of joyous celebration and of infernal, threatening delirium. Through de Segonzac's moderate temperament we glimpse a romantic, nostalgic intermixing of man and nature.

Fortunately, Provence offers much the same inventory of delights and attractions for the modern traveller as it did for visitors a century ago. It remains one of those few areas of Europe largely unaffected by the despoliation of the modern world.

THE MEDITERRANEAN COAST

The southern coast of the French landmass breasting the western basin of the Mediterranean, known generally as the Midi, falls into two main areas; the shoreline of the Golfe du Lion lying to the west of the river Rhône and, to the east, the great mass of Provence. In the extreme west the coastline rises northwards from the point where the eastern peaks of the Pyrenees meet the sea through the ancient, semi-autonomous Catalan region of Roussillon (see Mountains chapter), its capital, Perpignan, lying a few miles inland, tucked under the foothills of the Pyrenees and the limestone plateau of Corbières. The coast gradually curves round to the east in a broad arc to form the Golfe du Lion. The inner section of this enormous gulf, from the ancient Roman capital of Narbonne to the mouth of the Rhône some 150 miles (241 kilometres) away, is formed by the Languedoc coast. This is a broad alluvial apron which runs northwards to the limestone mountains of the Cévennes and the Massif Central. The coast is one of wide sandy beaches and, until recently, mosquito-plagued saltwater lagoons. For this latter reason the area was one of low population and few visitors until recent development was undertaken with an eye on the expanding package-holiday market. The marshes and lagoons have been drained, and high-rise developments have rapidly spread along the now sanitized beaches. The few towns and villages scattered along this littoral contain much evidence of their former importance, when the southern coast of France was the key to the nation's wealth. The *Canal du Midi*, built by Louis XIV to link Toulouse with the Mediterranean, meets the sea just west of Sète, formerly the leading French Mediterranean port after Marseilles. Montpellier is the regional capital, an ancient seigneurial seat. Some 30 miles (48 kilometres) inland to the north-east is the great textile centre of Nîmes, dominated by the extensive remains of the Roman aqueduct, the Pont du Gard. Towards the mouth of the Rhône lies the large salt marsh expanse of the Camargue, long associated with horse-breeding and bullfighting.

To the east of the Rhône, where the great arc of the Alps runs down to meet the sea, is the bluff prominence of Provence, which bulges south to the picturesque Iles d'Hyères before curving back to run along the north-eastern edge of the Ligurian Sea – the famous Côte d'Azur – which reaches the border with Italy just east of the principality of Monaco. The whole rocky protrusion is pitted with deep natural bays and harbours, the names of ports along Europe's oldest and most famous maritime resort familiar to all: Marseilles, originally a Greek colonial settlement and France's oldest port, La Ciotat, the great naval base of Toulon, Hyères, St Tropez, St Raphael, Cannes, Antibes, Nice, Villefranche, Monaco and Menton. It should not be forgotten that many of these now fashionable centres were once simply small fishing villages, sharing a closer kinship with their Italian neighbours along the Ligurian coast than with the fishing communities of the Languedoc beaches.

From classical times onwards many of these ports and their hinterlands all along the Mediterranean coast prospered from trade with the Italian ports of Genoa, Livorno, Naples and Venice, and formed part of a network which stretched throughout the Mediterranean and Black Sea, with entrepôts on the Anatolian, Levantine and Egyptian shores. They were integral links in a trading system which stretched from north-western Europe, via the Mediterranean, to the Middle East and beyond. In the ninth and tenth centuries these coastal communities were natural targets for the Norman and Arab pirates who ransacked the eastern Mediterranean, and for a time their wealth and security were seriously threatened. However, by the beginning of the twelfth century they were secure. Many of the ports were fortified and new garrison ports such as Aigues Mortes (1240), were built, many of which were embarkation ports for the Crusaders *en route* for the Holy Land. The area was itself the centre of another crusade, against the Albigensian heresy, which was brutally suppressed by the Capetian nobles of the north during the twelfth century.

A serious blow came in the seventeenth century, when the race for overseas colonies and the attendant development of an Atlantic economy robbed the region of much of its commercial importance. The pursuit of French imperialism in Africa (which was finally very considerable) did not really get underway until the second quarter of the nineteenth century; prior to that French energies were directed towards North America, the Caribbean and the Pacific. Thus immediate and rapid access to the Atlantic sea lanes, via the ports of the Channel coast, was the *entrée* to the world's stage; only with the consolidation of Algeria as a French colony in 1870 did the Mediterranean coast begin to reassume its early commercial and strategic importance. At the same time the development of tourism on an international scale opened up the region to a new form of industry – one which today pays most of the region's grocery bills.

Throughout the early modern period, when the economic and political hub of Europe shifted from the Mediterranean heartland to the younger, Protestant, states of the north-western seaboard, France, with its strong Catholic ties, still remained culturally oriented towards Italy and the lands of classical antiquity. It took a social and political upheaval as devastating as the French Revolution to alter this; it is interesting, therefore, that the artistic taste and style associated with the Revolutionary period – Neo-classicism – still sought to reinterpret the models of the classical past, but within a radical, modern ethic. Although a renewed taste for things classical was becoming fashionable in France some two decades before the Revolution of 1789, Neo-classicism subsequently focused on the political and ethical virtues of early Republican Rome as an anti-religious, pre-Catholic canon of values suitable for emulation in the modern world. This period of outspoken and idealistic reform was short-lived, giving way to a more pragmatic view of the contemporary world.

GUSTAVE COURBET
THE ARTIST ON THE SEASHORE AT PALAVAS,
1854
Musée Fabre, Montpellier

We have seen elsewhere how, in the nineteenth century, French painters began to look northwards, to the work of English, Dutch and German painters, and developed, through Naturalism, Realism and Impressionism, a new and iconoclastic style of art which allowed them to deal directly with the world about them. By the end of the century certain painters, Gauguin and Van Gogh notable among them, were becoming dissatisfied with the limited, superficial opportunities offered them by Naturalism and its direct progeny, Impressionism, and were seeking a means of defining in paint something more than the mere objective analysis, however aesthetically appealing, of outward appearances. For many artists this new impulse drew them away from northern climes: Van Gogh went to Provence seeking sunshine; Cézanne returned there, to his home, to work in peace and in the clear, uninterrupted light; Gauguin went further afield, seeking new stimulus in the alien and ancient cultural environment of French Polynesia.

The return to the south, to the Mediterranean light and climate and its potential associations with classical art, was not universally endorsed – nor did it bring the sort of results one might expect. The English art critics Roger Fry and Clive Bell wanted to see in it a definite return to classical values, especially in the work of Cézanne (see Provence chapter). This tendency, however, is more readily identifiable in the heroic classical motifs and figures which appeared in the work of Picasso and André Masson in the 1920s. The work of the artists who moved to the Mediterranean coast at the turn of the century seems now to have borne rather different fruit, having more to do with the immediacy and potency of light and bright colour under clear Mediterranean skies than with the classical preoccupations of form, modelling and structure. Cézanne himself summed up his reaction to the Mediterranean atmosphere after working in and around Paris for over twenty years: 'The sun is so terrific here that it seems to me as if the objects were silhouetted not only in black and white but in blue, red, brown and violet. I may be mistaken, but this seems to me to be the opposite of modelling.' Modelling had long been one of the keystones of classical art.

Cézanne often worked on the seashore of Provence, the small village of L'Estaque, on the edge of the Gulf of Marseille a few miles south of his home at Aix, being a favourite setting. He rarely painted the village close up, being more interested in the formal possibilities of richly pigmented terracotta roofs clustered on the seashore, facing a ridge of mountains across the bay. His viewpoint was usually from among the hills immediately behind the village. The slanting roofs, chimneys and occasional towers form an almost geometric pattern in the foreground, the oranges and light ochres broken only by the greens of tree-tops and patches of market garden and meadow; the middle ground is occupied by the expanse of seawater in the bay, rising to the richly worked horizon line formed by the land on the opposite shore.

Cézanne's L'Estaque pictures are suffused with light, the modelling of the various elements less ostentatiously worked with the brush than his other landscapes or still-lifes; however, as usual, there is little distinction in the size or quality of brushwork between foreground and background, what pictorial depth there is arising purely from the selection of colours.

For Cézanne the light and colour of the south were to act as catalysts in his struggle with modelling and form, his attempt to resolve the three-dimensional world with the two-dimensional canvas; for a group of painters known as the Fauves, some 20 years later, these features were to be a source of direct inspiration and liberation.

In the summer of 1904 the Divisionist painter Signac spent some weeks working with Henri Matisse (1869–

PAUL CÉZANNE
L'ESTAQUE AND THE GULF OF MARSEILLES,
1883–85
Metropolitan Museum of Art, New York

Painted shortly before his father's death, at a time when Cézanne was staying in Provence under something of a domestic cloud (due to his father's disapproval of his liaison with Hortense Fiquet), this brilliant canvas nevertheless shows the assurance Cézanne had gained as a *paysagiste* in the decade since he had taken up landscape painting under Pisarro's influence (see page 71). His interest in patterned brushwork and in the geometrical design of the elements of the composition here find a perfect equilibrium with the evocative rendering of the view in a traditional landscape sense. There is a feeling of liberation too, in the rich range of colours which could be used quite legitimately under the Mediterranean sun, and which is largely absent from the pictures Cézanne produced in and around Paris.

1954) at St Tropez. Signac's style had already broken free from the restraints of 'scientifically' analysed colour espoused by his mentor Seurat (see Introduction and Rivers chapters), and he allowed brighter and more adventurous colours to inform his Divisionist technique of applying paint. The result was essentially romantic in its evocation of scene and setting. For the young Matisse, the technique of building up a picture in small dabs of pure colour was stylistically limiting and rather stilted, but the experience of applying adjacent and sharply

PAUL SIGNAC
THE PORT OF ST TROPEZ,
1902
Collection Signac, Paris

The ironic link between Impressionism, the high point of naturalism in the arts, and the major abstract movements at the beginning of the twentieth century is here made explicit. Although Signac (above) adopted the Divisionist style developed by Seurat, his painterly qualities and genuine appreciation of landscape never allowed his style to become as dry and doctrinaire as that of his master. When the young Matisse spent a summer painting with Signac at his home in St Tropez in 1904, he began to emulate the *pointilliste* elements of the older painter's style. But where Signac used *pointillisme* as a means of building up a hazy, coloristically accurate representation of a view, Matisse accentuated the dislocation of the dots of paint, giving them a non-naturalistic patterning quality which helped to emphasize the mythical allusions of the composition. As in the later work of Cézanne (see page 128), we are confronted by the point at which the representation of a landscape gives way to the inner life and meaning of the painting as a separate object.

HENRI MATISSE
LUXE, CALME ET VOLUPTÉ, 1904–05
Private collection

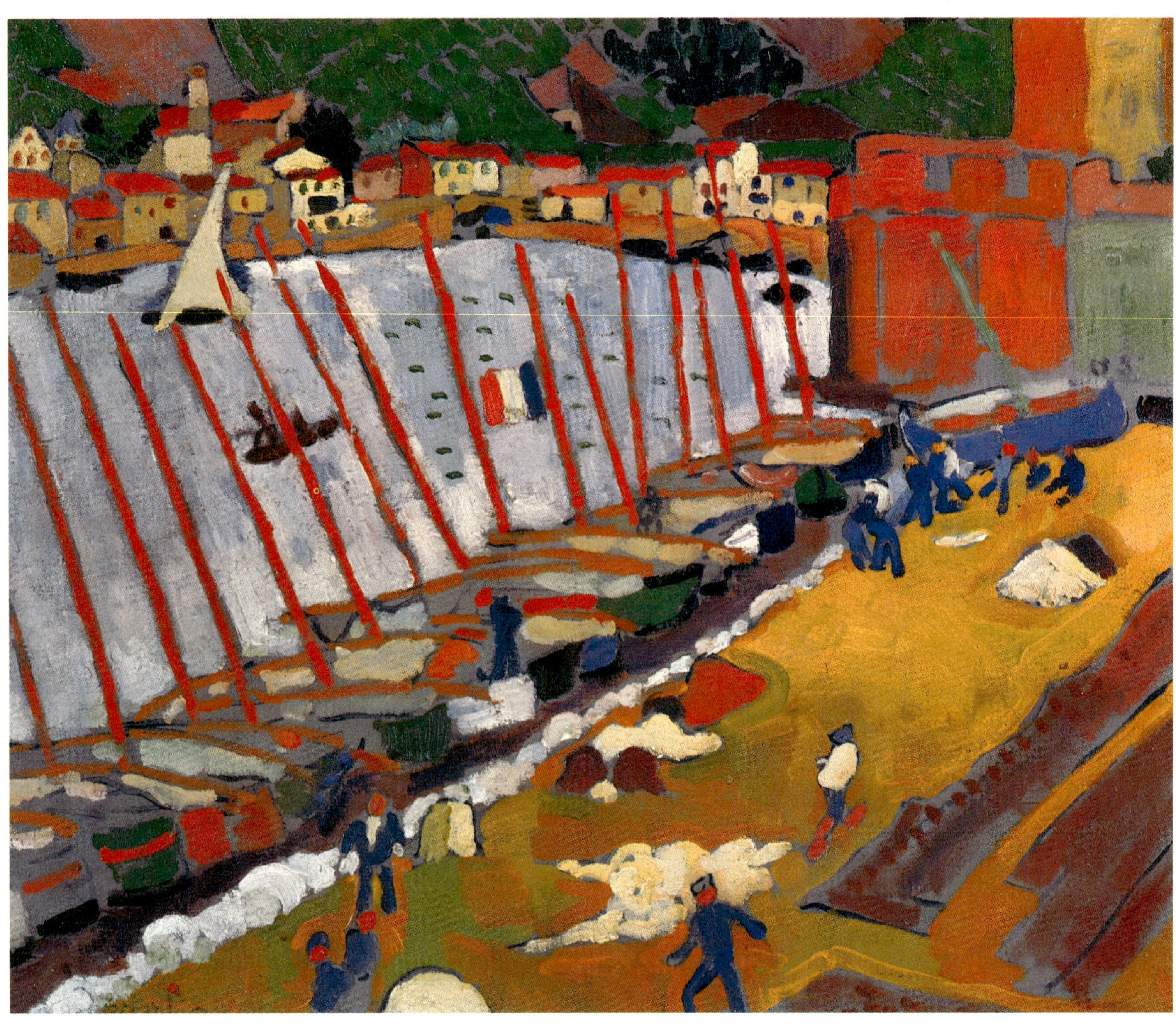

ANDRÉ DERAIN
THE HARBOUR AT COLLIOURE, 1905
Musée National de L'Art Moderne, Paris

contrasting dabs of pure colour on a clean, white canvas was dynamic. His painting *Luxe, Calme et Volupté* (1904–5) was exhibited at the Salon d'Automne in 1905. This was the third occurrence of an annual exhibition established by a group of independent artists and critics (including Renoir, Matisse and the Symbolist writer Huysmans) who were dissatisfied with the existing round of annual exhibitions. The first, in 1903, had been devoted to a memorial exhibition for Gauguin, the second a large retrospective of Cézanne's work. In 1905 the show included, along with that of Matisse, work by André Derain, Raoul Dufy, Maurice de Vlaminck and Georges Braque, all of whom seem to have taken a statement by Gauguin to heart: 'Instead of trying to render what I see before me, I use colour in a completely arbitrary way to express myself powerfully.' A critic at the 1905 exhibition, finding a restrained marble figure sculpture among so many exuberantly bright canvases, exclaimed: *'Donatello au milieu des fauves!'* (Donatello among the wild beasts), and the label stuck, although the group as such were only briefly united in their aims and interests. One strong bond among many of them, however, was their experience of painting in the Midi.

The central figure in the Fauve group remained Matisse, who rapidly outgrew the confines of his experience of painting with Signac. Matisse had trained in the late 1890s in the studio of the Symbolist and literary painter Gustave Moreau, who was noted for his subtlety and daring as a colourist. Among his fellow pupils were Albert Marquet and Georges Rouault, who were both later associated with the Fauves, the former working principally in Normandy (see Normandy chapter) and the latter rarely painting landscapes, concentrating rather on figure studies. In Paris in 1901, at an exhibition of Van Gogh's work, Matisse met Maurice de Vlaminck (1876–1958), who was to become one of the most outstanding and committed of the Fauve circle. His lifestyle closely matched the popular caricature of the 'modern' artist. Devoutly anti-intellectual, self-taught and outspokenly anti-establishment, he began his career as a racing cyclist, and spent some time as a travelling fiddler in the south of France. Vlaminck boasted that he had never set foot in the Louvre and stated: 'I wanted to burn the Ecole des Beaux-Arts with my cobalts and vermilions and I wanted to interpret my feelings with my brushes without thinking what had gone before.'

This was not strictly true, as the Van Gogh exhibition inspired both Vlaminck and André Derain to unleash pure, unmixed pigment on to their canvases directly from the tubes. The bright colours and sunlight of the Midi complemented Vlaminck's interests, and it is likely that the physical experience of blurred visual perception and the speeding impression of the form and colour of landscape which he gained as a competitive cyclist informed his work. His paintings are undoubtedly violent, and fit the temper of a time in modern history when Anarchism was in vogue (Vlaminck, in anarchistic form, once advocated arson as an acceptable means of political expression).

In many ways Vlaminck's approach and the results he achieved epitomize Fauve painting: his attempt to convey the greatest possible immediacy through the undisciplined use of colour moved beyond the representation of the subject before him into a conceptual realm. This in turn may be the reason why Fauvism existed so briefly – the idea could not maintain, or retain, a fresh style, and in the absence of any external formal discipline it lapsed easily into a mannered, programmatic and predictable approach. Vlaminck, unlike many of his fellow Fauves, remained largely unaffected by such developments as Cubism, although his later work acquired a greater sense of structure, largely through his study of Cézanne.

GEORGES BRAQUE
HOUSES AT L'ESTAQUE,
1908
Kunstmuseum, Berne

André Derain (1880–1954) was a less exuberant character and worked harder for his effects. He painted with Matisse at Collioure, in Roussillon, in 1905, and for both painters this was a summer not so much of formative influence (as had been 1904 for Matisse) but of consolidation and innovation. They spent the summer

HENRI MATISSE
LE LUXE, 1907
Musée National de L'Art Moderne,
Paris

moving away from the Divisionist technique espoused by Signac towards a more experimental approach to interpreting landscape in pure colour. Derain pursued something of the Divisionist technique, taking it to its logical conclusion in the seascape *Effects of Sunlight on Water* (1905). The resemblance to traditional land- or seascape here is established solely by the firm horizon line and the tonal range of colours, although the hues Derain employed are considerably exaggerated. The dark, heavy, simplified shapes of clouds are silhouetted against a burning evening sky (it is not quite sunset, the brightness of the sun being indicated quite high in the sky); as the towering clouds reach the horizon they blend with the blues and greens of the distant water and a spit of land which runs symmetrically across the canvas. We 'read' the foreground as water, or sea, because of the undisturbed reflection of the sun's light spreading across the surface towards us. Despite this naturalistic interpretation of the subject, the form and approach is very nearly abstract: the painting remains an exercise in the application of bright, contrasting colours and generalized shapes painted in numerous vibrant, jostling brushstrokes of equal size and shape, flattening the plane of the canvas. Derain later used what he had learnt about colour to freely distort more clearly naturalistic subjects, employing hot reds and yellows for highlights and emerald greens and royal blues for shadow. Unfortunately his enthusiasm for this inventive and expressive luminosity waned after a few short years, and his later work was more conservative.

Another experiment with Fauve colour can be seen in the work of Georges Braque, who flirted with the combination of Divisionist technique and non-naturalistic colour prior to his ventures, with Picasso, into Cubism. Born at Argenteuil but raised in Le Havre, he worked on the Provençal coast at L'Estaque and La Ciotat in 1906 (following a period at the Ecole des Beaux-Arts in Paris) with another Fauve enthusiast, Otto Friesz. His approach at this time involved the application of largely unmixed bright pigment in single brush strokes, but these were organized in such an apparently loose and disconnected way as to suggest the decomposition of the visual image (in direct opposition, that is, to the careful attempts of Seurat and Signac to build up a coherent image). Braque, however, retained a delicacy, sense of balance and composition which holds these pictures together, and which looked forward to the immensely controlled brushwork of early Cubism.

Of all these early twentieth-century explorers of the Midi coast, however, Matisse remains the most fascinating and significant, and the one figure among them who most nearly fulfilled the notion of a return to the classical

JUAN GRIS
LANDSCAPE AT CÉRET, 1913
Nationalmuseum, Stockholm

world of the ancient Mediterranean. In the years following his encounter with Signac, Matisse painted with Vlaminck and Derain on the Côte d'Azur and in close proximity to Braque. Matisse too moved away from the initial lessons of Divisionism towards a method of painting which dealt more directly with pure colour in a less fussy manner. In doing so, his work evolved along two parallel paths. On the one hand, in a range of studies of the village of Collioure, we can see individual brush strokes merging into broader, flatter areas of colour, the details of houses and even of mountains picked out in rudimentary notations of rose and vermilion, set against a limited range of bright greens.

On the other hand, Matisse worked around the conspicuously traditional notion of a landscape with nude figures, with strong overtones of a classical, mythical subject. If the nude figures in *Luxe, Calme et Volupté* could be seen simply as bathers, gathered as they are on a Mediterranean beach, sunbathing or drying their hair, the scene presented in *Bonheur de Vivre* (1905–06) is more overtly Arcadian in its references. The protagonists are arranged in discrete groups, pursuing a range of sensual pleasures from music-making and dancing to love-making and languorous relaxation. They are all nude, and are set in a wooded landscape which opens on to a beach with a distant band of sea. We understand the climate and atmosphere to be hot, conducive to nakedness. The composition is held together by a series of darkly incised arabesque curves and by areas of bright colour washes; grass and branches are indicated by almost calligraphic single brushstrokes. The whole effect is uncomplicated and unselfconscious – a long way from the determined iconoclasm and shock tactics used by Manet in his 'modern idyll', *Déjeuner sur L'Herbe*, some 40 years beforehand (see Introduction).

Matisse was to develop this Arcadian theme over the next decade; *Luxe, Calme et Volupté* was to be reworked twice (1907 and 1908), refining the original version down to a composition of three monumental female nudes set in a beachscape, which was described in six simple blocks of unmodulated colour. Later, Matisse took the distant group of dancers in *Bonheur de Vivre* and worked them up to form the basic design of one his most famous paintings, *The Dance* (1910), in which five bright red figures form a rhythmic, linked pattern in the simplest of all landscapes – blue sky and green ground.

RAOUL DUFY
NICE AT SUNSET
Private collection

We can see here a very different outcome from the first phase of Fauve painting in the Midi. The wild rejoicing in a liberated palette which marked the work of Matisse, Vlaminck and Derain in 1904–5 had been transformed into a cool and contemplative exercise in harmonious control and balance, not only of extraordinary colours, but also of shapes. The traditional dichotomy between form on the one hand, and colour on the other (which was the basis of the nineteenth-century confrontations between Classicism and Romanticism) was resolved; in Matisse's work both concerns are prominent, but neither is dominant. In fact, it is the equilibrium which he achieved between colour and form which epitomizes Matisse's most significant work. His landscapes painted in North Africa immediately before the Great War, the series of *Odalisques* of the 1920s, the still lifes and portraits of his inter-war years all developed this notion of balance and interaction; a preoccupation which eventually led to the sublime simplicity of his paper collages of the 1940s and 1950s.

Another dichotomy in the arts which emerged towards the end of the nineteenth century was between the extreme naturalism of the progressive Impressionists and Divisionists and the more literary and historical interests of the conventional academic school of painting; this was also resolved in Matisse's work. Much of his subject matter was undeniably classical or traditional – but the manner in which it was dealt with was undeniably modern.

Matisse remains one of the two or three giants of twentieth-century painting, and no small part of his achievement was due to the geographical locale of much of his working life. It is not true to say, however, that the bright colours and luminosity of Fauvist painting was dependent solely upon a Mediterranean setting. After all, Marquet worked primarily in Normandy, and Derain produced some equally colourful pictures of Paris and, surprisingly, London. However, it is fair to say that the first Fauvist works were greatly influenced by the artists' experience of the Midi, and it is tempting to link the iconoclastic daring and rejection of convention in these works to the kind of lazy, bucolic, sun-drenched idyll that many today associate with their summer holidays. The languid, unselfconscious nudes of Matisse's *Luxe* series could not really exist anywhere but in a Mediterranean climate, yet they relate as much to Arcadian demigods of classical myth as to the modern sun-worshippers who yearly flock to the beaches of the Midi.

Other painters were attracted to the Midi for a variety of reasons. The Spanish painters Juan Gris (1887–1927) and Pablo Picasso (1881–1973) both worked there, presumably due to the area's proximity to their home-

NICOLAS DE STAËL
COMPOSITION, 1951
Kunstmuseum, Basel

land. The latter spent most of his later years there, often producing variations on classical themes (in a manner not dissimilar to Matisse), although rarely working in landscape. Gris, who shaped Picasso's enthusiasm for Cubism, produced some vivid landscape canvases in which bright colour almost completely subsumes the analytical concern with form which underly his Cubist works.

The strength of colour revealed by the Mediterranean sun which seems to have been a potent catalyst for many of the artists we have looked at, often drawing them away from traditional representation towards increasing abstraction, found its most poetic and extreme interpreter in the Russian painter Nicolas de Staël (1914–55). His family emigrated to Brussels (where he trained) via Poland, and he settled in France in 1937. He became a close friend of Braque, and under his influence in the 1940s began to establish his own characteristic style. He applied thick, usually rectilinear, blocks of paint in subtly varied colours, placed in careful juxtaposition, building up an abstract equivalent for the direct experience of colour and texture in nature. Landscapes, especially those of the Midi, Morocco and Sicily, were his usual starting point, although his early paintings bear little obvious resemblance to their source. After 1950, the influence of Cubism can be increasingly traced as pure abstraction was gradually rejected and vaguely recognizable forms began to appear in his work, often arranged along and before a clear horizontal division resembling a skyline. Like Gris before him, de Staël's raw material was colour, and out of his brilliant and resounding hues arises a strong evocation of the joy of nature. His success can be measured by the uncomplicated reaction to nature and the landscape which his paintings convey. His work, though abstract, is not difficult to approach or appreciate.

Sadly, de Staël, like many contemporaries such as Pollock and Rothko, found the struggle to realize his vision an unequal one. He committed suicide aged only 41.

There is one painter whose work defies pigeon-holing into any particular group or school, but whose work for many embodies not only the local atmosphere and colour of the Côte d'Azur but the kind of lifestyle popularly associated with it. Raoul Dufy (1877–1953) began his career in Le Havre and Paris, working in a decorative, Impressionist manner, but this style was soon rejected as he enthusiastically embraced the explosion of colour values of Fauvism, which remained the strongest influence on him. The work for which he is most fondly remembered bears little of the passion and vehemence of his Fauvist years, however. His paintings became highly representational, specific views realized in a peculiar combination of bright colour washes with areas of artificial white highlight, over which Dufy worked a kind of calligraphic notational shorthand, picking out details of form and shape in black and pure primary colours. The style today has been much emulated and is similar in effect to silk-screen printing, which has done much to cheapen Dufy's achievement – although it says much for the successful immediacy of his style. Few, however, can capture his mastery of economic, evocative draughtsmanship with a brush, or indeed his daring and control of apparently incompatible colour washes.

Dufy's decorative paintings capture the spirit of the Côte d'Azur – the pleasures of the well-to-do, with marinas full of elegant yachts, the bright lights of cafés glittering on the dusky surface of the harbour and days divided between the seashore and the saddle. He also recorded the period during which the Midi was transformed from the string of quiet fishing resorts enjoyed by Cézanne, Signac and Matisse to the modern centre of one of Europe's most profitable industries – tourism.

The painters of the Mediterranean coast brought French landscape painting full circle. The Arcadian vision which Claude and Poussin sought to discover among the ancient ruins of Rome was reborn in southern France in this century. On the face of it, any similarity between the sirens who crowd the beaches at Antibes and Cannes and the goddesses of classical myth might be a difficult one to swallow; yet it is no accident that the three greatest artistic figures of the century, Cézanne, Matisse and Picasso, whose achievements have dominated modern painting, all produced their finest work – work of great variety, innovation and historical awareness – here, on the southern shores of France.

BIOGRAPHICAL NOTES ON THE ARTISTS

EMILE BERNARD

1868–1941

Friend and associate of Gauguin, Van Gogh and Cézanne. Originally working in the Divisionist style, he destroyed all these paintings following an argument with Signac. In 1886 he was in Brittany, where he met Gauguin, and was impressed by the latter's work. Bernard developed a style similar to Gauguin's Synthetism, which he called *Cloisonnisme* because of its dependence upon contours with rich flat colour infills. He later felt that Gauguin received too much credit for the Pont-Aven style, and they quarrelled. He spent eight years travelling in Europe and the Near East, and his later works became less adventurous and increasingly religiose.

Above Bernard

RICHARD PARKES BONINGTON

1802–1828

Born near Nottingham, his family moved to Calais in 1817; he was familiarized early with both lithography and with English watercolour technique. He entered the Ecole des Beaux-Arts in Paris in 1820, trained under the leading Romantic, Gros, and was a friend of Delacroix. He experimented with the exotic historicism of contemporary French Romanticism, but also developed a delicate and fresh landscape style in watercolour, exhibiting examples of the latter at the *Salon* of 1822, and in the 'English' *Salon* of 1824. In that year he travelled to England with Delacroix, there seeking work by Constable, whose influence can be seen in his later paintings. The spontaneity and effectiveness of his *plein air* watercolour and oil sketches remain his greatest legacy. He died of tuberculosis before his 26th birthday.

PIERRE BONNARD

1867–1947

The early associate of the Nabis painters Vuillard and Denis, he re-introduced a fervent appreciation of Japanese prints into French contemporary art, emphasizing asymmetric composition and the use of strong contours containing rich areas of colour and patterning. After 1900 his style became more painterly and Impressionistic, still relying on rich colours, but blending them into a thick impasto. With Vuillard, he developed *Intimisme*, a style characterized by undramatic, sensual subject matter and the exploitation of surprisingly bright, decorative colour. His deceptively simple prints were enormously influential upon later painters.

EUGÈNE BOUDIN

1824–1898

A great influence on the Impressionists, Boudin lived and worked for most of his career in one of their favourite landscapes – Normandy. He was born at Honfleur, and was encouraged by Millet to take up painting, displaying his pictures in his framing shop. He was taught for a time by the marine painter Isabey, but his unique, detailed technique and peculiar luminosity in recording the beaches and skies of Normandy places him as a transitional figure between the naturalists of the Barbizon School and the true Impressionists. He greatly influenced the young Monet and his work was included in the first Impressionist exhibition, which was held in (1874).

Above Bonnard

GEORGES BRAQUE

1882–1963

Trained as a specialist decorator, this experience in gaining effects with paint remained an essential advantage in Braque's career as one of the great painters and teachers of the twentieth century. A Belgian by birth, he studied at the Ecole des Beaux-Arts in Le Havre, and later in Paris, where he began to experiment with Fauve techniques. He soon met Picasso and began experimenting with the flattened surfaces and disjunctive compositional forms which ultimately led to Cubism. In 1908 he exhibited a series of views of L'Estaque which synthesize Fauve colour and the elements of decorative Cubist form. He continued to develop Cubism with Picasso through all its primary stages, including one introduction of collage techniques. He served in the Great War (1914–18), and subsequently (like Picasso) developed away from Cubism towards a proliferation of highly painterly styles of increasing sophistication.

PAUL CÉZANNE

1839–1906

Probably the most influential painter of the last century, Cézanne only began to receive recognition late in his career. Born the son of a prosperous Provençale tradesman and financier, he went against his father's wishes (and followed his friend, Emile Zola's advice), when he abandoned the study of law for a Parisian painter's life in 1862. Here he developed an arch Romantic style of great vigour and little subtlety. He returned to the family home in L'Estaque during the Franco-Prussian War (1870–71), but in 1872 joined Pissarro (whom he met in the 1860s) at Pontoise where he began to paint closely-observed pure landscapes. During the 1870s he gradually moved, under the Impressionists' influence, away from his Romantic style of painting, towards a new and laborious method of reconstructing the scene before him in a dialectic of pure colour and form. Landscape

Left Braque

remained a principal pursuit for the rest of his life, although he applied similar artistic principles to many still-lifes and to portraits and figure paintings. He exhibited at the first Impressionist exhibition in 1874, but continued public and critical abuse made him very reclusive. In 1886, upon his father's death, he finally withdrew to the family home at Jas de Bouffon near Aix. The same year Zola published *L'Oeuvre*, in which Cézanne saw a defamatory portrait of himself, thereafter severing relations with the writer. In 1890, he was invited to exhibit by Les XX in Brussels. In 1895 he had his first large exhibition. During the last ten years of his life he turned to large-scale ambitious figure subjects (*The Bathers*), whilst continuing an extraordinary series of paintings of Mont Ste Victoire. He died after developing pneumonia shortly after being soaked in a rainstorm whilst painting *en plein air*.

CLAUDE (LE) LORRAINE
1600–1682

With Poussin, the principal landscapist of the Roman Baroque school, Claude was born in Lorraine, but moved to Rome aged 12. In the 1620s he worked in Naples for two years, and the dramatic landscape of the region remained central to his vision of the classical world. In 1625 he returned to Lorraine and here applied some of the formal principles of the Italianate landscape to paintings of local scenes. He returned to Rome in 1627, where he remained, developing an increasingly enveloping and convincing poetic vision of a harmonious and conspicuously classical landscape world. Always representing an historical or mythological scene (often drawn from Virgil) his figures remain small in relation to their setting, intrinsically part of the world they inhabit.

Commissioned in 1639 to paint two landscapes for Pope Urban VIII, his reputation was thereafter assured. Often remembered for the serene cohesion of his style, and his use of a suffusing, rather artificial light, Claude was not afraid to introduce unusual dynamic elements – unusual landscape forms, dramatic contrasts in scale, bravura expanses of open water – to achieve his ends.

Left Cézanne

Above Claude Lorraine

JEAN BAPTISTE CAMILLE COROT
1796–1875

The most influential French landscape artist of the first half of the nineteenth century. Corot's work bridged the gap between the Academic tradition of the classical landscape and the intense naturalism of the Impressionists. He was born in Paris, and trained under Bertin and Michallon, visiting Italy, via Switzerland, in 1825–27 to complete his classical training. He worked in and around Rome, where by painting *en plein air* he introduced a new immediacy and lively palette to the classical landscape programme. He travelled extensively in France until 1834 (returning to Italy twice in 1833 and 1834) and these travels are recorded in numerous drawings and oil sketches, realized in a free and expressive technique.

By the 1850s, he had developed a formal style of idyllic landscape using a hazy nostalgic lighting scheme, which became immensely popular and earned him Academic recognition. Within and around the core of this rather contrived style, Corot managed to produce some fascinating tonal essays prefiguring Whistler, and studies of the play of light and shadow comparable with Degas. He lived at Ville d'Avray for the last twenty years of his life, making it something of a cult centre. He was lauded by artists of the younger generation, and did much to plead their case with Academic jurors. Known for his generosity, he helped support both Daumier and Millet in their later years. An immensely productive artist, examples of his work can be found in most major museums and galleries, and in many provincial collections. Corot's popularity has also made him one of the most forged artists.

Above Corot

GUSTAVE COURBET

1819–1877

The most notorious painter of the Realist movement, and a formidable landscapist. Courbet was born at Ornans in the Jura. In Paris from 1840, he was largely self-taught, copying the Old Masters in the Louvre and working at the Atelier Suisse. Vigorously anti-intellectual, he concentrated on a broad range of subjects – nudes, still-life, portraits, sea and landscapes – drawn from everyday life but which, like Manet, seemed to both refer to and criticize established artistic tradition and practice.

His paintings of peasant life, *The Stonebreakers* (1849) and *Burial at Ornans* (1850), established his reputation and identified him as a man of the Left. He unwisely involved himself in radical politics following the 1848 revolution and during the 1871 Commune, leading to his eventual imprisonment and subsequent exile in Switzerland where he died. Following his *L'Atelier du peintre* (1855), a kind of painted philosophical statement of his beliefs and values, in which he indicated his prime role as a landscapist, his paintings became less vociferous and concentrated increasingly on an intense observation of various French regions.

Left Courbet

Above Daubigny

CHARLES FRANÇOIS DAUBIGNY

1817–1878

With Corot, the most important peripatetic painter of the French landscape in the first half of the nineteenth century. He trained formally under Paul Delaroche, and exhibited at the *Salon* from 1848. He consistently painted *en plein air*, although his style carries something of the quality of the Dutch Baroque School. Often associated with the Barbizon School (although he never lived at Barbizon), his work stretched beyond both their geographical and formal limitations. He travelled throughout France, often working from his 'floating studio', as well as visiting England, the Netherlands and Italy. His informal style and intuitive handling of water as a transitional medium between the solid world of form and the transparent world of light was immensely influential upon the Impressionists.

EUGÈNE DELACROIX

1798–1863

For many the high-priest of the Romantic movement in French painting, but Delacroix's enormous *oeuvre* consistently belies popular notions of Romanticism in his advocation of drawing as a basic structural skill, his selection of literary and historical subject matter and his numerous large-scale formal projects. Delacroix's Romanticism is a result of his great skill as an innovative colorist, his interest in dynamic form and movement, and owes a debt to his public profile as a flamboyant, sexually adventurous loner.

Unfortunately his work in landscape was limited, although landscape backdrops to offset figure paintings such as *The Massacre at Chios* (1824) reflect his understanding of the English School of Turner, Bonington and Constable whom he admired. His importance in creating a taste in France for the work of both the Netherlandish Baroque School and the English Romantics is only equalled by his significance as a figurehead of French Romantic painting in the middle years of the nineteenth century.

Right Delacroix

ROBERT DELAUNAY

1885–1941

Credited as the inventor of Orphic Cubism, his early preoccupation with Impressionism led him to return to a series of immobile Parisian landscape motifs (notably the Eiffel Tower) which he used as a formal basis for exercises in geometrical colour harmonies. He exhibited in 1911 with the Independents, and with the *Blaue Reiter* group. He worked in Spain and Portugal (1914–21), but returned to Paris, where he was commissioned in 1937 to paint a series of murals for the Universal Exhibition. His wife Sonia was also an influential painter.

ANDRÉ DERAIN

1880–1954

One of the original Fauves, Derain's spectacular use of colour was a hallmark of his work until c. 1914. His first major influence was Cézanne, from whose work he gained a feel for structure and brushwork, but the influence of Vlaminck and Matisse brought out the colorist in him. He worked in Paris, the Midi coast and London, investing all locations with irrationally bright colours. In his later work he became less dramatic, continuing to favour landscapes, but in more traditional earth colours.

Left Derain

ALEXANDRE FRANÇOIS DESPORTES

1661–1743

Trained in the Flemish Baroque tradition, Desportes worked as a portraitist before becoming official painter of hunting scenes to both Louis XIV and Louis XV. Although famed for his pictures of game, hounds, and other animal portraits and still-life, the background landscape sketches he prepared for these formal works remain early masterpieces of *plein air* painting. Desportes was occasionally commissioned to paint private country houses, which gave him greater range to display his gifts as a landscapist. He was influential in introducing a taste for Flemish art into France. Many of his paintings can be seen in the Louvre.

NARCISSE VIRGILE DIAZ DE LA PEÑA

c.1807–1876

Trained as a porcelain painter. Diaz carried a taste for pastoral idylls over into his early canvases – landscapes populated by bathers, shepherdesses and gypsies. In 1837 he met Rousseau, and began to paint pure landscape, deploying his considerable fluency as a painter to new and creative effect in the rendering of light and atmospheric conditions. From the 1840s he figured as a central figure of the Barbizon School, although he also painted on the Biscay Coast.

RAOUL DUFY

1877–1953

The most consistently successful exploiter of Fauve techniques, and one of the Godfathers of 'modern' graphic aims and methods. He began his career emulating the Impressionists, but under the influence of the Fauves he began to use brighter colours applied in broad irregular areas, laying, or drawing, almost calligraphic notations over them to build a picture. His subject matter was mainly restricted to the social life of the Riviera and Paris, and his style matched perfectly the lightweight, decorative characteristics of his subject. Dufy also designed ceramics and textiles, and was a great influence on the fashion world of his time.

Below Dufy

PAUL GAUGUIN

1848–1903

Important Post-Impressionist painter whose development of Synthetism greatly influenced the development of abstract art. Born in Paris, he spent part of his childhood in his mother's native country, Peru. He became a stockbroker in 1871 although he was an amateur painter and collector of Impressionist works. His early works were Impressionist in style, and it was from their expressive brushwork and heightened colour that his later style began to develop. Gauguin left the stockmarket to paint full-time in 1883, placing his family life under great pressure. He eventually separated from his wife and moved from Paris to Brittany, living at Pont-Aven and Le Pouldu, where his peculiar insight into earthly spirituality and a formal resolution of abstract themes began to take root and to suggest ideas.

A highly influential group of like-minded painters coalesced around him at Pont-Aven. His interests were broad ranging, and his use of features derived from Japanese, Polynesian, African and Romanesque art set him well ahead of his imitators.

He visited the Caribbean (1887) and spent two terrible months painting with his friend Van Gogh in Provence (1888). His irascible nature, persistent impecunity and taste for bodily pleasures coloured his artistic life. In 1891 he went to Tahiti, returning broke to France in 1893, and whilst in Brittany was involved in a brawl (1894). He returned to the South Seas in 1895, where his final years were dogged by poverty, illness and harassment from the colonial authorities due to his support for various native causes. Gauguin's work shows a clear, stage-by-stage development, achieving a considerable maturity in each phase.

JEAN-LÉON GÉRÔME

1824–1904

A notable Academic painter and sculptor, Gérôme studied under Delaroche, and continued through his career to uphold the Academic tradition, opposing a gift of Impressionist pictures to the Luxembourg. His work was extremely popular, partly due to his immensely refined technique. By the end of the century his style had reached such a peak of heightened realism that it bore comparison with some of the work of the Symbolists. His principal preoccupation was with historical and classical subject matter.

Right Gauguin

VINCENT VAN GOGH

1853–1890

Dutch painter of landscapes, portraits and still-life whose development of expressionist colour, composition and brushwork was profoundly influential on twentieth-century artists. He was born the son of a Dutch pastor, and began his career working for an art dealer, at first in The Hague, London and then in Paris. He threw up his career to teach, and finally became a pastoral missionary in the Borinage mining region of Belgium. This vocation he was forced to give up, and was a vagrant for some months before taking up art full-time. From 1880–86 he worked and trained variously in Holland and Belgium, developing a brutal realist style for rendering scenes of poverty and social injustice. In 1886, he stayed with his brother Theo in Paris, and came into contact with Impressionism. For two years he refined a technique derived from Impressionism, but in which the selection of colours and combination of brushmarks had more to do with the artist's instinctive reaction than with objective observation. Compositionally, like the Impressionists, Van Gogh was heavily influenced by Japanese prints. In 1888 he moved to Arles in Provence to escape from Paris. He had hoped to find an artists' commune. Gauguin visited him for two months, and perceived in his manner and work intense depression and mental instability. Certainly his style in Provence wavered between solidly constructed, firm compositions and wild, expressively animated canvases. In December 1888 he admitted himself to an asylum for the insane, and from then until his suicide at Auvers-sur-Oise he suffered regular bouts of mental instability and produced paintings at frenzied speed.

JUAN GRIS

1887–1927

Spanish painter, in Paris from 1906, where he fell under the influence of fellow countryman Picasso. By 1911 he was working in a Cubist manner, attempting to imbue natural or found objects with a geometrical order and solidity. His vivid colour sense became of central importance after 1913, and his experiments with collages contributed to the development of synthetic Cubism. He produced still-life, illustrations and stage sets as well as painting landscapes.

CARL FREDRIK HILL

1849–1911

Swedish landscape painter whose work in France (he lived in Paris for several years during the 1870s) showed a very different development from the emulation of Corot to that followed by the Impressionists. His ability to capture mood in a classical sense aligns him with Corot, but his increasing practice of *en plein air* painting led him through the intensively realistic representation of observed reality towards a form of Expressionism. Hill lost his sanity in 1878, but continued to produce telling landscape images in coloured chalk.

VICTOR HUGO

1802–1885

French novelist, poet and dramatist, Hugo was a central figure in the Romantic movement in the arts. He also worked in the graphic arts, producing drawings and watercolours in a highly expressive manner. His style developed after a visit to the Rhineland in 1840, and he produced pictures when living in Luxembourg and towards the end of his life in Normandy and the Channel Islands. His pictures have an historical quality, and murky atmosphericism.

Left Van Gogh

Left Manet

JOHAN BARTHOLD JONGKIND
1819–1891

A Dutch landscape and marine painter whose work in France had a great influence on the young Impressionists. Oddly, he worked from watercolours and sketches and never painted in oils *en plein air*, but the looseness and immediacy of his technique impressed Monet. He exhibited at the *Salon des Refusés* in 1863, and spent his later life in poverty near Grenoble, drinking heavily and eventually going mad.

THE LIMBOURG BROTHERS, Pol, Hennequin and Herman
active 1400-c.1416

Employed by the Duke of Burgundy from 1411, they became the court painters of the Duke of Berry. Their background is unclear, but it seems that some at least trained as goldsmiths in Paris, and later were imprisoned in Brussels, and released after a ransom had been met by the Duke of Burgundy. Their two major commissions for the Duke of Berry, *Les Belles Heures* (by 1413) and *Les Très Riches Heures* (unfinished by 1416) remain masterpieces of the International Gothic style. The success of these illuminations relies on an exquisite balance between high stylization, precisely handled colour and draftsmanship, and a fresh observation of nature, the landscape and the human activities within it.

EDOUARD MANET
1832–1883

His bourgeois parents disapproved his choice of career, and although Monet trained under the leading Academician Couture, he reacted against traditional history painting, turning at first to genre realism, then to a series of radical reinterpretations of traditional themes; these were realized in a unique style of carefully juxtaposed areas of paint with little half-tone modulation. In these he worked directly from the model in a vigorous, direct fashion. This phase culminated in the notorious *Dejeuner sur l'Herbe* (1863) and *Olympia* (1865). His consistent rejection from the *Académie Salons* (on the grounds of crude technique) led him to be a focus for the next generation of artists, and his work formed the principal centrepiece of the *Salon des Refusés*. Both Baudelaire and Zola voiced their support for him, and Monet most neatly fits the former's requirements for a 'Painter of Modern Life'. Under the influence of younger admirers such as Renoir, Berthe Morisot, and Monet in the later 1870s, he painted increasingly *en plein air*, but although his work acquired Impressionist characteristics, he remained an admirer of formal composition. He yearned for official recognition and refused to exhibit with the Impressionists.

ALBERT MARQUET
1875–1947

Trained in the studio of Moreau, Marquet there met Matisse and Rouault, and was associated with their coloristic and formal experiments which led to the development of Fauvism. He was never as committed as the rest of the

His career followed, if possible, a process of increasing reduction of detail, reaching a final point of resolution in his primary colour collages of the late 1940s and 1950s. His work was undeniably decorative in effect, whilst profoundly intellectual in motivation; his mythic landscape was inextricably bound up with the shores of the Mediterranean.

CHARLES MERYON

1821–1868

A leading architectural print-maker, Meryon worked at a time, and in a milieu, which allowed his views of Paris to epitomize the Romantic era in that city. The illegitimate son of an English doctor and a French dancer, he joined the French navy and travelled in the South Pacific where he produced some paintings and drawings. By 1849 he was in Paris, and began a series of etchings of the city, varying in subject from straight, though atmospheric, renderings of buildings and docks, to feverish visions of the city infested with strange flying beasts, animated gargoyles and scurrying, fleeing figures. The series proved unpopular, although it was admired by Hugo, Gautier and Baudelaire. His colour-blindness restricted him to monotone print-making. The unsettling quality of his work reflected his private life: from 1858–59 he was in an asylum, and in 1866 he was committed again, where he remained until he died.

group to the use of harsh colours, and preferred to develop a Post-Impressionist style of landscape founded upon the articulation of massed blocks of unmodulated colours. This style developed into a relatively simple, almost decorative technique, which he used for a range of landscapes, seascapes and townscapes.

HENRI MATISSE

1869–1954

The leader of the Fauve group, and one of the most influential painters of the twentieth century. He trained under the Academician Bouguereau and under the Symbolist Moreau, in whose studio he met Rouault and Marquet. He met Vlaminck and Derain in 1901, whilst working under the influence of Cézanne. The experience of working with Signac on the Mediterranean coast (1904) produced strong works of both formal and coloristic confidence. From this point Matisse abandoned strict representation in favour of themes which best suited his pictorial ideas, most marked in the reduction of form to contoured simplifications, and colour to carefully balanced fields of rich contrasting tones. Landscape was always an important feature of Matisse's work, but like his abstract ideals, it remained subservient to his primary interest in the human form.

Above Matisse

GEORGES MICHEL

1763–1843

Originally a picture restorer, working on the Dutch and Flemish collection at the Louvre, Michel learnt much from the Baroque masters and was a major conduit introducing their influence to French landscape painters in the first half of the nineteenth century. He consistently painted *en plein air* (unlike the Old Masters) and it is this which gives his paintings a greater and more immediate freshness than those of his forebears. Although he exhibited regularly at the *Salon* from 1791–1821 he enjoyed little popular success until his work was discovered by the Barbizon School.

JEAN-FRANÇOIS MILLET

1814–1875

Born of peasant stock in Normandy, he trained under a local artist before going to Paris to study under Delaroche (1837). His early work is marked by a sentimental pastoralism and eroticism. In 1848 he exhibited his first peasant subject, and thereafter became increasingly committed to the representation of the rural poor and the agricultural landscape rendered with enormous pathos and monumentality. In 1849 he moved to Barbizon, where he worked for the rest of his life, only occasionally returning to Normandy, or visiting the Auvergne (recommended for his wife's health). His rather prosaic style of painting is belied by his facility as a draftsman and print-maker.

CLAUDE MONET

1840–1926

The leading member of the Impressionist group, and the most consistent practitioner of the basic tenets at the heart of the movement. Monet was born in Paris, but spent his childhood in Le Havre, where he met and worked with Boudin, who persuaded him to become a landscape painter. In 1859 he went to Paris, working at the *Atélier Suisse*, where he met Pissarro. He was in military service in Algeria (1860–62) thereafter returning to Paris, where he met Jongkind, and also at the studio of Gleyre the contemporaries who would, with him, forge Impressionism: Bazille, Sisley and Renoir. He worked variously and widely with them, always *en plein air*, as he later did with Courbet, Whistler, Manet and Cézanne. His paintings were notable for their extraordinarily bright palette and vivid rendering of light. In the late 1860s and again in the mid-1870s he spent lengthy periods painting with Renoir at La Grenouillère and Argenteuil on the banks of the Seine, sessions during which their disintegrated brushwork and perception of colour as a medium of light coalesced. During the Franco-Prussian war of 1870–71 he worked in London; in 1872, at Le Havre, he painted *Impression: Sunrise* which inadvertently provided the public with a name for his style of naturalism.

In later years Monet created a home at Giverny (1883), where he began to paint a series of variations on certain themes – haystacks, poplars, Rouen Cathedral – painting the same subjects in different shades of light. In 1889 he began the ambitious water-lily paintings, based on his own garden, which he continued to work at, with failing sight, until the end of his life.

Below Monet

LOUIS GABRIEL MOREAU

1739–1805

French landscape painter whose sensitive and delicate handling of the nuances of landscape, foliage and atmosphericism presaged the naturalism discovered by French nineteenth century painters. He never enjoyed the popularity of Robert or Vernet, and indeed moved beyond their rather picturesque style in creating a heroic landscape similar to popular contemporary painting in Germany.

PAUL NASH

1889–1946

One of the leading British Surrealists, Nash remains among the finest European landscapists of the century. His experience of battle during the Great War (during which he was wounded) inevitably affected his outlook. He was created an Official War Artist in 1917 (and again during the Second World War), and his best known paintings record with heightened distortion the destructive power of warfare on the landscape. The work of the European Surrealists and of the Metaphysical artists influenced him strongly in the inter-war years, and his poetic vision often dwelt upon isolation and the irrational power of peculiar natural forms. He founded the avant garde British association Unit One, and produced many fine book illustrations.

JOHN PIPER

1903–

British painter and designer. A leading abstract painter during the 1930s, by the beginning of the Second World War (in which he was an Official War Artist), under the influence of Surrealism, he reverted to naturalism especially in representations of the landscape. During the war he recorded the effects of the war on the British landscape and townscape. During the 1950s he was much involved with design work, and a new interest in abstraction appeared in his landscapes at the end of the decade.

CAMILLE PISSARRO

1831–1903

Born in the West Indies, of mixed parentage, he worked in his father's store before going to Venezuela in 1852 with a Danish painter. Thereafter his parents accepted his career, and he travelled to Paris in 1855, mixing with the Realists there, but also falling under the influence of Corot. He concentrated on landscape painting, and in 1859 met Monet; he exhibited at the *Salon des Refusés* in 1863. He lived at Pontoise (1866–69), working in the open air on landscapes (often with peasant figures). As for Monet, Cézanne and Sisley, this was an impoverished period. He went to England during the Franco-Prussian war (1870–71) and returned to find many of his canvases destroyed. In 1872, Cézanne worked with him at Pontoise, a particularly fruitful period for both artists. Pissarro exhibited at all eight of the Impressionist exhibitions. During the 1880s he was increasingly influenced by Seurat's quasi-scientific theories of Divisionism, and adapted his style to that method. Consistently experimental, he was central to the Impressionist group, and remained friendly with all its principal figures. His eldest son, Lucien (1863–1944) was also a notable painter, whom he and other Impressionists taught.

Above Pissarro

NICOLAS POUSSIN

1594–1665

Born in Normandy, and training under the leading court painter Philippe de Champaigne, Poussin went on to become the leading painter of Baroque Rome. He arrived in Rome in 1624 and worked under Domenichino. After five years working in the competitive milieu of Counter-Reformation Italy, and following a serious illness, he turned from large-scale religious subjects to smaller-scale classical works, from which he developed an austere, dramatic and carefully balanced formal style, realized in carefully controlled colours and delicate planes of light and dark. He returned to France in 1640 at the invitation of Cardinal Richelieu, but after 18 unhappy (and unpopular) months he returned to Rome for good. Poussin's principal style involved carefully wrought figure groups set in overtly contrived architectural or landscape settings bearing obvious classical traits. His archaeological and literary interests led him toward an increasing economy of style, monumentality of form and reduction of dramatic colour and light effects. His 2 *Seven Sacrament* series (1642 and 1648) are philosophical and psychological masterpieces of modern classicism. In later years his interest in landscape increased, and *The Seasons* (1664) reveal a resurgence of poetic feeling in place of the often chilly rationalism of his middle years.

PIERRE AUGUSTE RENOIR

1841–1919

One of the greatest and most popular of the Impressionists. He worked from 1854 in a china factory, giving him a solid foundation in decorative, luminous painting. In 1861 he was working in Gleyre's teaching studio, where he met Monet, Bazille and Sisley. He was also impressed by the works of the Old Masters in the Louvre, especially Rubens, Watteau, Boucher and Fragonard. There is a strong strain of tradition throughout his work. During the 1850s he worked in the manner of Courbet, using heavy impasto, but working from nature. But his work painting landscapes with Monet – most especially at La Grenouillère in 1868 – was decisive, his tone and palette becoming lighter and looser. He exhibited at the first three and the seventh Impressionist exhibitions, and enjoyed greater success at the *Salons* than his fellow Impressionists. Always more interested in people than in landscapes, his views are nearly always populated, and he was the greatest of the school at rendering bustling street scenes in Paris.

His interest in the figure led him to develop a more classically informed style where form – especially the portrait or the female nude – was accorded equal emphasis with the traditional interests of the Impressionists – light and colour. In 1906 he moved to the Midi coast, but was inhibited in his work by arthritis. During the last years of his life he was friendly with Matisse, and supported some of the ideas behind Fauvism. He was a prolific painter, producing about 6,000 pictures.

HUBERT ROBERT

1733–1808

Studying in Rome from 1754, and a friend of the Romantic ruin-painters Piranesi and Panini, Robert introduced this style into France, and enjoyed great success. In 1761 he travelled to Sicily and southern Italy with Fragonard. In 1765 Robert became a member of the *Académie* and continued to earn a substantial living painting views in and around great country houses, including Versailles. He later became keeper of the King's Pictures, and Curator of the Louvre, which today contains much of his work. His unique contribution to French painting remains his development of a fresh, spontaneous style of street genre painting, showing everyday life in the byways of Paris.

Above Renoir

THÉODORE ROUSSEAU

1812–1867

Painting *en plein air* from an early age, Rousseau enjoyed early success when his paintings of the Auvergne were exhibited in 1832. Largely untrammelled by tradition, he approached the problems of landscape painting boldly and expressively, resulting in his consistent rejection from the annual *Salon*. '*Le grand refusé*' thus earned a cult reputation among younger artists, and when, in 1848, he settled at Barbizon, he attracted a considerable circle of admirers and followers, including Millet, Diaz and Daubigny.

Above Rousseau

ANDRÉ DUNOYER DE SEGONZAC

1884–1974

Working first as a Cubist, his work as a camouflage-designer during the Great War seemed to draw him towards naturalism, and in the 1920s he joined the *Bande noir*. He worked in still-life as well as landscape, his oils being worked in heavy impasto, but his watercolours and etchings revealing a much lighter touch. He became a leading bastion of naturalism during the most intense anti-naturalistic period of the century, and also illustrated books.

PAUL SÉRUSIER

1863–1927

As a young man, he met Gauguin in Brittany in 1888, and there developed a form of Synthetist painting which verged on abstraction. *The Talisman* (1888), a landscape painted under Gauguin's guidance, remains one of the first masterpieces of modern art. Based in Paris, Sérusier formed the Nabis group with Bonnard, Vuillard and Denis. Their style drew upon certain superficial elements of Impressionism and the symbolic qualities of the Pont-Aven school to produce bright, highly decorative works. Their inability to find a suitably stimulating source of subject matter – interiors, nudes and sidewalk scenes remained their staple – made their work rather insubstantial. Sérusier went to Germany in 1897, and stayed at a Benedictine monastery at Beuron, where he was influenced by various religious art theories. He published *ABC de la Peinture* in 1921, a rather outmoded text expounding certain quasi-Symbolist ideas.

GEORGES SEURAT

1859–1891

Leading Post-Impressionist painter, whose development of Divisionism (or Neo-Impressionism) created a unique and immediately identifiable style. He studied at the Ecole des Beaux-Arts, there studying the colour theories and practice of Delacroix, and Chevreul's book on the theory of colour. The aesthetic observations of Charles Henry, and David Sutter's experiments with vision and optics also influenced him, all these factors leading to the theory of Divisionism, where colours, reflected colours and colour contrasts were broken down into their constituent pigments and applied to the canvas in a series of tiny dots – a style of painting known as *pointillisme*. Seurat's sensitivity towards tone and nuances of light are revealed by his many preparatory drawings in charcoal, and his methodical development of his programmatic new style into a grandiose and highly polished statement: *Bathers at Asnières* was exhibited in 1884 at the *Salon des Indépendants*. He then developed a theory of proportion and composition, based on the Golden Section, which imposed an unfortunate rigidity on his already stiff style: his combined aesthetic viewpoint was summed up in *La Grande Jatte* (1886), which was shown at the last Impressionist exhibition. His later work showed him gradually moving away from the arch formal restraints of his two great paintings. Despite the conceptual nature of his theories, he always advocated working from nature, but ironically the publication of his ideas in 1890 greatly influenced the development of certain abstract artists and movements.

PAUL SIGNAC

1863–1935

A close follower of Seurat, Signac remains one of those unsung heroes of modern painting – the formidable formative influence. He exhibited with Seurat at the *Salon des Indépendents* (1884), which he helped to found. He soon adopted the *pointilliste* technique developed by Seurat, and although in theoretical writings such as *From Delacroix to Neo-Impressionism* (1899) he supported the quasi-scientific approach of Seurat, in his own work his palette became expressively bright, and his compositions more spontaneous. From

Above Signac

1892 he was based at St Tropez (where Matisse among others visited and worked with him), although he also sailed and painted extensively on both French coasts, and on the inland waterways.

ALFRED SISLEY

1839–1899

Born in France of English parents, he was sent to England to begin a commercial career (1856), but returned to Paris in 1862 and entered the Ecole des Beaux-Arts, meeting Monet, Bazille and Renoir. The following year he exhibited at the *Salon des Refusés*, and thereafter continued to paint landscapes in a consistent and increasingly Impressionist style. He exhibited at the first Impressionist exhibition (1874), having spent the Franco-Prussian war in England (1870–71).

Apart from his London pictures, his work dwells exclusively on Paris and its environs, at all times of year and in a great variety of weather conditions. Unique among the Impressionists in being comfortably supported by his family in his formative years, the family lost their money in the 1870s, and thereafter he had to struggle against public distaste for his style, and only began to enjoy any success just before he died.

CHAIM SOUTINE

1894–1943

Russian-born painter, in Paris from 1913. He shared a studio with Modigliani and was in the circle of various expatriate painters, and *peintres maudites* such as fellow-countryman Chagall, and Utrillo. He was heavily influenced by German Expressionism and probably by Van Gogh (although he disavowed the latter), developing a dense impasto style in a livid palette. In Paris he concentrated on still-life and portraits, the latter being exceptionally moving. He spent two periods working in the south of France in the 1920s, where he applied his style to landscape with great effect. He returned to Céret in the Pyrenees during the Second World War, to escape persecution as a Jew, where he died of a perforated ulcer.

NICOLAS DE STAËL

1914–1955

Born in Russia, and raised in Poland and Belgium, de Staël trained at the *Académie des Beaux Arts* in Brussels (1932–33). He settled in France in 1937, where he developed a pure abstract style related to the perception of land- and cityscapes. These remain exercises in the organization of freely painted blocks of colour, arranged to provide a synthesis of the experience of light and colour in the natural world. During the war he met Braque, and under his influence more recognizable landscape forms began to appear in his work. De Staël travelled widely, and his characteristic work was produced in Paris, the Midi coast, the Mahgreb countries and Sicily. In the 1950s the tension in his work between abstract and representational form, and between the use of pure primary colours and unmixed blacks and whites reached a kind of crescendo. He committed suicide aged 41.

Below Soutine

J M W TURNER

1775–1851

The leading British Romantic painter, and probably the greatest (certainly the most prolific) painter of landscapes Britain has produced. He was admitted to the Royal Academy Schools in 1789 at the age of 14, first exhibited at the Royal Academy in 1791, became an Associate in 1799, an Academician in 1802 and Professor of Perspective in 1807. He was made Deputy President in 1845. In 1792 he made the first of many sketching tours which would provide his main source of material. Initially a topographic watercolourist, he began work in oil in the mid-1790s. He travelled extensively during the next 45 years, painting and sketching prolifically, and seeing at first hand canvases by Poussin and Claude. He knew France well, and visited Switzerland and Italy (1819, 1828, 1835 and 1840).

MAURICE UTRILLO

1883–1955

The illegitimate son of Suzanne Valadon, a painter and a model for Degas and Renoir, Utrillo was raised in the artistic milieu of Montmartre. His mother encouraged him to paint as a therapy for his alcoholism and drug abuse. His paintings are almost exclusively town views, possibly influenced by postcards, but retain a unique feel for painterly tonality and for urban loneliness. His best work belongs to his 'White Period' (c.1909–1916), so-called because of the pale tones which dominate the paintings. After this, success led him to a rather programmatic and repetitive style, using less carefully balanced colour schemes, that are nevertheless lively.

Below Vlaminck

Above Utrillo

LOUIS VIVIN

1861–1936

A leading French modern primitive or naive painter, he conformed to the 'Sunday painter' soubriquet in that he worked for the French post office, and painted as a pastime. His uniquely styled and colourful views of Paris were probably influenced by postcards. At the age of 61 he retired to paint full time, and was 'discovered' by the German critic Wilhelm Uhde, who exhibited his work in 1928.

MAURICE VLAMINCK

1876–1958

A prolific painter, notable as one of the Fauve group, Vlaminck was heavily influenced by the Van Gogh retrospective exhibition in Paris in 1901. He began to work in vivid colours, often using paint unmixed from the tube. He shared a studio with Derain, met Matisse, and exhibited with them at the *Salon d'Automne* in 1905. He was an admirer of African primitive art, although he denounced Cubism. His colourful background as a musician, racing cyclist and anarchist seems to have had a tangible influence on his work. Throughout his career he continued to paint landscapes, although his palette gradually became less bright.

EDOUARD VUILLARD
1868–1940

A formative member of the Nabis group, with Sérusier and Denis, his subsequent career paralleled that of his co-*Intimiste*, Bonnard. His work tends to be more decorative in impulse and effect than that of Bonnard, and he embraced a flat patterning effect derived from Japanese prints. Like Bonnard, after c.1900 his style became more painterly and naturalistic.

JEAN ANTOINE WATTEAU
1684–1721

Born in Valenciennes (in an area of Flanders recently conquered by Louis XIV), his style remained closely related to the Flemish tradition of genre peasant rural scenes, whilst typifying a particular aspect of French aristocratic urban life at the beginning of the seventeenth century. He arrived in Paris c.1702, and worked as a painter of theatrical scenes. In Paris he was influenced by the Rubens cycle *The Life of Marie de Medicis* and by the Venetian collections there. His principal works, including his Diploma work for acceptance to the *Académie des Beaux Arts, Embarkation for the Island of Cythera* (1717) are *fêtes galantes*, elegantly contrived scenes of contemporary fantasy, toying with notions of love, nostalgia, game-playing and theatrical characters. His significance as a landscapist resides in his evocation of the poetic worlds of Claude and Rubens within the experienced world of Parisian parks and gardens. He died from tuberculosis, from which he had suffered most of his adult life.

Above Vuillard

JAMES ABBOTT McNEILL WHISTLER
1834–1903

American painter, wit and dandy whose life and work in Europe epitomize the Aesthetic movement in the second half of the nineteenth century. Born at Lowell, Mass. and educated at West Point, he was a Navy cartographer before going to Paris in 1855 to study painting. There he met Fantin-Latour, Courbet and Degas. In 1859 he moved to London. He exhibited alongside Monet at the 1863 *Salon des Refusés*. The central theme of his work was the delicate balance between closely related colours and tones, and his paintings were often called Nocturnes or Symphonies.

Like the Impressionists, he found landscape the best subject for his experiments. In 1877 he sued the English critic Ruskin, who had accused him of 'throwing a pot of paint in the public's face' with his canvas *Nocturne in Black and Gold*. Whistler won the case but was awarded only one farthing damages, which led to his bankruptcy. He had to resort to his considerable skill as a graphic artist to recoup his losses. Whistler travelled widely in Europe, and visited South America.

INDEX

Page numbers in *italics* refer to illustrations

A

Abbate, Niccolō dell' 22
ABC de la Peinture 168
Abstraction 110, 121, 153
  Cézanne, P. 135–6
  Piper, J. 124
Académie des Beux-Arts 23, 25, 27, 41, 47, 61
agriculture 9, 11, 13, 16, 93, 96, 126
Allegory of Good and Bad Government (Lorenzetti) 18
Altdorfer, Albrecht 22
Alycamps, Arles, Les (P. Gauguin) *134*
Alycamps, Arles, Les (V. Van Gogh) *133*
Angelus, The (J-F. Millet) 58, *58*
Après Diner à Ornans, L' (G. Courbet) 90
Artist on the Seashore, The (G. Courbet) *141*
Artist's Studio, The (G. Courbet) 90
Ascanius and the Stag (C. Lorraine) *12*

B

Bal Champêtre, Le (J.A. Watteau) *13*
Bande noir 167
Banks of the Oise, The (C. Pissarro) *71*
Baptism of Christ (P. della Francesca) 18
Barbizon School 26, 27, 50, 55–6, 61, 66, 77, 78, 154
Bathers at Asnières (G. Seurat) 84
Battle of the Issus, The (Altdorfer) 22
Baudelaire, Charles 26, 42, 44
Beach at Bas-Butin (G. Seurat) *105*
Beach at Sainte-Addresse, The (J.B. Jongkind) *102*
Belles Heures, Les (Limbourg brothers) 18
Bernard, Emile 121, *123*, 154, *154*
Bertin 157
Bonheur de Vivre (H. Matisse) 151
Bonington, R.P. *19*, 26, 99, 101, 154
"Bonjour, M. Courbet!" (G. Courbet) *89*
Bonnard, Pierre *43*, 47–8, 121, 154, *154*
Bonvin, François 118
Boucher, François 38
Boudin, Eugène *98*, 101, 117
Braque, Georges 48, *147*, 149, 155, *155*
  Normandy 108, *109*, 110
Bridge at Mantes, The (J.B. Corot) *79*
Bridge at Narni, The (J.B. Corot) 78
Burial of Phocion, The (N. Poussin) *10*

C

Café at Night, The (V. Van Gogh) *131*, 139
Callot, Jacques 22, 65, 66
Campin, Robert 21
Carracci, Annibale 22
Cathedral of Notre-Dame, The (L. Vivin) *45*
Cézanne, Paul 27, 28, *28*, 47, 61, 79, *127–9*, 139, 142, *143*, 146, 153, 155
  Pontoise 70, 71
  Provence 129–30, 132
Charlemagne 8, 18, 32
Charles IX 22
Charles X 41
Chateau at Vandien (V. Hugo) *21*
Chateaubriand, F-A-R, 99
Chevreul 168
Church of Sacre Coeur, The (M. Utrillo) *49*
Church of Saint-Germain l'Auxerrois, The (C. Monet) *35*
Classicism 22, 24–25, 27, 90
  Mediterranean 142, 151, 153
Claude (Le) Lorraine *see Lorraine*
Claude Monet in his Floating Studio (E. Manet) *24*, 81, 83
Cloisonnisme 154
Coast of Brittany (J. M. Whistler) *113*
Coast of Brittany, The (J. Piper) *125*
Composition, 1951 (N. de Staël) *152*
Concert in the Tuileries gardens (E. Manet) *34*, 44
Constable, John 25–6
Corot, Jean Baptiste *33*, *60*, 61, 78, *79*, 79, 100, 157, *157*
Cottage Destroyed by an Avalanche, A (J.M.W. Turner) *87*
Cottet, Charles 123–4
Country Road by Night (V. Van Gogh) *137*
Countryside, The (T. Rousseau) *52*
Courbet, Gustave 26, *88*, *89*, 90, *91*, 93, 102, *141*, 158, *158*
Couture 163
Cozens, Sir Arthur 90
Cozens, John Robert 90
Cubism 48, 149, 153, 155
Cubism, synthetic 162

D

Dance, The (H. Matisse) 151
Daubigny, Charles 56, *76*, *77*, 78–9, 117, 158, *158*
Daumier, Honoré 42–3
Degas 44, 47
Déjeuner sur l'Herbe (E. Manet) *23*, 27, 44, 151
Delacroix, Eugène *20*, 26, 159, *159*
Delaroche 161, 165
Delaunay, Robert *41*, 47, 159
Delaunay, Sonia 159
Demolition of the Houses on Pont Notre-Dame (H. Robert) *31*
Denis, Maurice 121, 123, 154
Derain, André 48, *146*, 147, 149, 151, 159, *159*
Desportes, Alexandre François *64*, 65, 160
Diaz de la Peña, N. *54*, 55, 114, 117, 160
Dining Room with a View (P. Bonnard) *43*
Directoire 14, 38
Divisionism 28, 47, 70–1, 118, 136, 149, 166, 168
Divisionist style 154
Domenichino 167
Dufy, Raoul *150*, 153, 160, *160*
Dunoyer, André, de Segonzac, *see Segonzac*
Dupré, Jules 55
Dying Stag, The (G. Courbet) 93

E

Eaux-fortes sur Paris (C. Meryon) 42
Effects of Sunlight on Water (A. Derain) 149
Eiffel tower 47
Eiffel Tower, The (R. Delaunay) *41*, 47
en plein air painting 26, 56, 61, 66, 71, 78, 79, 81, 102
England, influence of 9, 25, 55, 90, 99–100
  topographic artists 38, 66
Estaque, L' (P. Cézanne) 142
Estaque and the Gulf of Marseilles, L' (P. Cézanne) *143*
Expositions Universelles 47, 90
Expressionism, German 169

F

Fantin-Latour 171
Fauvism 47, 48, 108, 110, 142, 146–7, 149, 151, 153

Filiger, Charles 121
Flight into Egypt (Carracci) 22
Floods at Port Marly (A. Sisley) *7*, *70*
folk tradition 11, 89, 121, 126–7, 129
Fontainebleau 11, 22, 37, 50, 53, *53*, 55, 61
forests 9, 11, 13, 50, *53*, 55, 126, 135
Four Poplars (C. Monet) *110*
Fragonard, Jean Honoré 25, 38
Francesca, Piero della 18
Francis I 11, 21, 22, 53
French Revolution 9, 14, 37, 38, 55, 141
Funeral at Ornans (G. Courbet) 90

G

gardens and parks 11, 13–14, 18, *19*, 25, *32*, *42*, 44, 47, *51*, 117
Gardens at Versailles, The (H. Robert) *51*
Gare St Lazare (C. Monet) *36*, 47
Gauguin, Paul 28, *115*, *116*, *118*, *119*, 139, 141, 142, 160–1, *161*
Brittany *120*, 120–1,
Provence 123, *134*
Géricault, Théodore 26
German Expressionism 169
Gérôme, Jean-Léon *82*, 161
Girtin, Thomas 99
Gleaners, The (J-F. Millet) 58
Gleyre 167
Gogh, Vincent Van *see* Van Gogh
Grande Jatte, La (G. Seurat) *27*, 84
Grandes Baigneuses, Les (P. Cézanne) *28*, 135
Grands Misères de la Guerre, Les (J. Callot) 22
Grenouillère, La 79, 83
Grenouillère, La (C. Monet) *69*
Grenoillère, La (P.A. Renoir) *68*
Gris, Juan *149*, 151, 153, 162
Gros 154
Guys, Constantin 44
Gypsies Going to a Fair (N. Diaz de la Peña) *54*

H

Harbour at Collioure, The (A. Derain) *146*
Harbour in Normandy (G. Braque) *109*
Haystacks (C. Monet) 107–8, 117
Henry II 22
Henry IV 37, 53
Hill, Carl Fredrik *67*, 162
Hills of Menton, The (L.G. Moreau) *17*
Houses at L'Estaque (G. Braque) *147*
Huet, Paul 55
Hugo, Victor *21*, 42, 100, 162

I

Ile Lacroix, Rouen (C. Pissarro) *106*
Impression: Sunrise (C. Monet) 102, *104*, 105
Impressionism 28, 44, 66, 78, 79, 83, 84, 102, 110
use of colour 56, 101
In the Auvergne (J.F. Millet) *92*
Ingres, Dominique 26
International Gothic style 18, 21
Intimisme 154
Isabey, Eugène 100, 154
Italy, influence of 18, 22, 25, 26, 38, 121, 127, 129

J

Jacob wrestling with the Angel (P. Gauguin) 118, 121
Japan, influence of 47, 117, 121, 136
Japanese prints 154
Jetty at Deauville, The (E. Boudin) *98*
Jongkind, Johan Barthold 101, *102*, 163

K

Kandinsky, Wassily 108

L

Landscape (F. Desportes) *64*
Landscape at Céret (J. Gris) *149*
Landscape Study in the Forest of Fontainebleau (T. Rousseau) *53*
Landscape with Rocks and Trees (P. Cézanne) *127*
Landscapes as background 18, 21, 89
Les XX 156
Life of Marie de Medicis, The 171
Limbourg brothers *9*, 18, *75*, 89–90, 163
Loue Valley with a Gathering Storm, The (G. Courbet) *88*
Lorenzetti, Pietro 18
Lorraine, Claude (Le) *12*, 22, 24, *63*, 65–6, 90, 156
Louis IV 50
Louis VI 11
Louis VII 11
Louis XIII 22, 38, 50, 53
Louis XIV 11, 25, 38, 53, 62, 74, 114, 171
Louis XV 55
Louis Napoleon 44, 47
Louis-Philippe 41
Louvre on a Snowy Morning, The (C. Pissarro) *37*
Luncheon of the Boating Party, The (P.A. Renoir) *39*
Luxe, Calme et Volupté (H. Matisse) *145*, 146, 151
Luxe, 1907, Le (H. Matisse) *148*

M

Manet, Edouard *23*, *24*, 27, *34*, 43–4, 81, 102, *103*, 163, *163*
Mannerism 22
Marquet, Albert *46*, *85*, 108, 147, 151, 163
Masson, André 142
Matisse, Henri 142–3, *145*, 146–7, *148*, 149, 151, 153, 164, *164*
Maufra, Maurice 121
Meryon, Charles *32*, 41, 42, 164
Michallon 157
Michel, Georges 56, *57*, *164*
Mill near Brighton (J. Constable) 26
Mill on a River (C. Lorraine) *63*
Millet, Jean-François 26, 56, 58, *58*, *59*, 61, *92*, 93, *97*, 165
Modernism 27–8
Mona Lisa (L. da Vinci) 21
Monet, Claude 28, *35*, *36*, 47, 61, 66, *69*, 79, 81, *101*, 102, *104*, 105, 107–8, *110*, *111*, 117, 118, *124*, 165, *165*
Monet in his Floating Studio (E. Manet) *24*
Morisot, Berthe 79
Mont Ste Victoire (P. Cézanne) *128*, *129*, 135–6
Moreau, Gustave 147, 166
Moreau, Louis Gabriel *17*
Morgue, The (C. Meryon) *32*
Moulin de La Galette (V. Van Gogh) 26
Mountain Hut, The (G. Courbet) *91*
Mountain Pasture, The (J-F. Millet) 93

N

Nabis 47, 121
Nabis painters 154, 168, 171
Napoleon I, 14, 38, 41
Napoleon III 27, 41
see also Louis Napoleon
Nash, Paul *73*, 166
Naturalism 27, 101, 141
Neo-Classicism 38, 41, 141
Neo-Impressionism *see* Divisionism
Netherlands, influence 25, 55, 100
Nice at Sunset (R. Dufy) *150*
Night Café, The (V. Van Gogh) 138–9

O

O'Conor, Roderic 123, 124
October (Limbourg brothers) *75*
Oeuvre, L' (E. Zola) 132
Old Bridge, The (H. Robert) *15*
Olympia (E. Manet) 44
On the Banks of the Seine (M. Vlaminck) *40*
Orpheus and Eurydice (N. dell'Abbate) 22
Orphic Cubism 159
Otto I 18

P Q

Panini 167
Park at Versailles, The (R.P. Bonington) *19*
Peasant Cottage at Gruchy (J-F. Millet) *97*
Philip II (Augustus) 32
Philip IV 50
Philippe de Champaigne 167
Picasso, Pablo 48, 142, 151, 153
Piper, John 124, *125*, 166
Piranesi 167
Pissarro, Camille 27, *37*, 47, 61, 66, 70–1, *71*, 79, *80*, *106*, 130, 166, *166*
Pissarro, Lucien 166
Pointillism *see* Divisionism
Pond at St. C . . . , The (J-L. Gérôme) *82*
Pont Aven (E. Bernard) *123*
Pont Aven School 47, 120–1, 123–4
Pont Aven style 154
Pool with Herons (C. Daubigny) *77*
Poplars (C. Monet) 107
Port of St Tropez, The (P. Signac) *144*
Post-Impressionism 47
Pouldu, Le (P. Gauguin) *120*
Poussin, Nicolas *10*, 22–4, 167
Primaticcio, Francesco 22
Public Garden (E. Vuillard) *42*
Quai Conti under Snow (A. Marquet) *46*
Quai Orfevres, Paris, Le (J.B. Corot) *33*

R

Rape, The (P. Cézanne 129–30
Realism 26, 27, 56, 90, 102
Red Roofs (C. Pissarro) 70
Renoir, Pierre Auguste *39*, 44, 47, 61, 66, *68*, 79, 81, 167, *167*
Return from Cythera (Watteau) 25
Richelieu, Cardinal 167
Road from Grimaud, The (A. Dunoyer de Segonzac) *138*
Roadstead at Boulogne (E. Manet) 102, *103*
Robert, Hubert *15*, *31*, 38, *51*, 55, 167
Rocks by the Sea (P. Gauguin) *115*
Romanticism 26, 27, 41, 42, 55
Roofs (N. de Staël) *29*
Rouault, Georges 147
Rouen Cathedral (C. Monet) 107, 108, *111*, 117, 165
Rough Sea at Belle Ile (C. Monet) *124*
Rousseau, Henri (Le Douanier) 48
Rousseau, Théodore *52*, *53*, 55, 61, 100, 168, *168*
Royal Academy, Turner at the 170

S

St George and the Dragon (Altdorfer) 22
Salon d'Automne 146
Salon des Refusés 27
Second Empire 44
Segonzac, André Dunoyer de *138*, 139, 168
Séguin, Armand 121
Seine at Asnières, The (P. Signac) *81*
Seine Landscape (C.F. Hill) *67*
Sérusier, Paul 121, *122*, 168
Seurat, Georges *27*, 28, 47, 84, *105*
Sickert, Walter 118
Signac, Paul 28, *81*, 118, 142–3, *144*, 168, *168*
Sisley, Alfred *7*, 61, *70*, 83, 168, *169*
Snow Storm: Hannibal and his Army Crossing the Alps (J.M.W. Turner) 90
Snow-covered road at Honfleur (C. Monet) 102
Snow Scene (P. Gauguin) *116*
Soutine, Chaim 47, *94*, 95, 169, *169*
Sower, The (J-F. Millet) 58
Spirituality 121
Spring (J-F. Millet) *59*, 61
Staël, Nicolas de *29*, *152*, 153, 169
Starry Night (J-F. Millet) 61
Stevens, Alfred 123, 124
Still Life with Lobster (E. Delacroix) *20*, 26
Storm, The (G. Michel) *57*
Sunflower series (V. Van Gogh) 136
Surrealism 48
Sutter, David 168
Symbolism 22, 47, 61
Synthétisme (Synthetism) 121, 123, 154, 160

T

Talisman, The (P. Sérusier) 121, *122*
Terrace at Sainte-Addresse (C. Monet) *101*
Third Republic 37, 41
topography 5, 18, 25, 38, 55, 61, 90, 100–1, 126
tourism 14, 16, 25, 47, 48, 93, 141
Très riches heures, Les (Limbourg brothers) *9*, 18
Turner, J.M.W. 25–6, *87*, 90, 105, 170

U

Uhde, Wilhelm 170
Unit One 166
Universal Exhibition 159
Urban VIII, Pope 156
Utrecht Psalter 18
Utrillo, Maurice 48, *49*, 170, *170*

V

Valadon, Suzanne 170
Van Gogh, Theo 162
Van Gogh, Vincent 26, 28, 47, *72*, 75, 141–2, 162, *162*
Oise 71–2
Provence 123, 129, *130*, *131*, *133*, 136, *137*, 138–9
Vernet, Horace 100
Versailles 14, *19*, 25, 38, *51*, 53, 55, 61
View of Céret (C. Soutine) *94*
View of the Seine (C. Pissarro) *80*
View on the River Marne (A. Marquet) *85*
Village Stream, The (C. Daubigny) *76*
Ville d'Avray (J-B. Corot) *60*
Vinci, Leonardo da 18, 21
Virgil 156
Virgin of the Rocks, The (L. da Vinci) 21
Vision after the Sermon, The (Jacob wrestling with the Angel) (P. Gauguin) *118*, 121
Vivin, Louis *45*, 48, 170
Vlaminck, Maurice de *40*, 48, 79, 147, 170, *170*
Voyages pittoresques et romantiques dans l'ancienne France 100
Vuillard, Edouard *42*, 47–8, 121, 171 *171*

W

warfare 8, 9, 14, 16, 22, 43, 62, 86, 89, 99
Waterlily series (C. Monet) 108
Watteau, Jean Antoine *13*, 25, 38, 171
We are making a new world (P. Nash) *73*
Weyden, Rogier van der 21
Wheatfield, 1890 (V. Van Gogh) *72*
Wheatfields at La Crau, near Arles (V. Van Gogh) *130*
Whistler, James McNeill 27, 47, *113*, 117, 171
Winnower, The (J-F. Millet) 58

Y Z

Yellow Haystacks, The (P. Gauguin) *119*
Zola, Emile 129, 132, 155, 156

ACKNOWLEDGEMENTS

The publishers would like to thank the following for their permission to reproduce their material in this book.

2	The Metropolitan Museum of Art, New York
9	Musée Condé, Chantilly
10	The Earl of Derby, Knowsley, Lancashire
12–13	The Ashmolean Museum of Art and Archaeology, Oxford/The Bridgeman Art Library
13	Collection Viscomte de Neailles
14–15	National Gallery of Art, Washington DC
16–17	Paris, Louvre/Giraudon
18–19	Paris, Louvre/Cliché Musées Nationaux
20–21	Paris, Louvre/Giraudon
21	Maison de Victor Hugo/Photo Bulloz
23	Musée d'Orsay, Paris
24	Bayerische Staatssammlung, Munich
27	Helen Birch Bartlett Memorial Collection, 1926.244, © 1987 The Art Institute of Chicago. All Rights Reserved
28	The Philadelphia Museum of Art
29	Paris, Musée National d'Art Moderne
30–31	Paris, Musée Carnavalet/Giraudon
32	The Board of Trustees of the Victoria and Albert Museum
32–33	Paris, Musée Carnavalet
34	The Trustees, The National Gallery, London
34 below	Paris, Collection Juvala
35	Nationalgaleri, Berlin
36	Paris, Musée d'Orsay
37	The Trustees, The National Gallery, London
39	Phillips Collection, Washington DC
40–41	Collection Buhrle Schalk, Zurich
41	The Philadelphia Museum of Art
42	Paris, Musée National d'Art Moderne
43	The Minneapolis Institute of Art
44–45	Musée d'Art Moderne de la Ville de Paris
46–47	Collection Marquet, Paris
49	Museu de Arte de São Paolo
50–51	Musée de Versailles
52	Barletta, Museo Civico, Gallerie de Nittis
53–3	Paris, Louvre
54	Bequest of Susan Cornelia Warren, Museum of Fine Arts, Boston
56–57	Wilson L Mead Fund, 1935.374 © 1987 The Art Institute of Chicago. All Rights Reserved
58	Paris, Louvre
59	Paris, Louvre
60–61	National Gallery of Scotland
62–63	Seth K Sweetser Fund, Museum of Fine Arts, Boston
64–65	Musée National du Château de Compiègne
66–67	Nationalmuseum, Moderna Museet, Stockholm
68	Nationalmuseum, Moderna Museet, Stockholm
69	The Metropolitan Museum of Art, New York
70	Musée d'Orsay, Paris
71	Private Collection
72–73	Stedelijk Museum, Amsterdam
73	The Trustees of the Imperial War Museum, London
75	Musée Condé, Chantilly
76	The Metropolitan Museum of Art, New York
77	Paris, Louvre
79	Paris, Louvre
80	Private Collection
81	Paris, Collection Signac
82–83	Richard Green Collection, London
84–85	Musée d'Art Moderne de la Ville de Paris/Giraudon © DACS 1988
86–7	The Tate Gallery, London
88–89	Musée des Beaux-Arts, Strasbourg
89	Musée Fabre, Montpellier/The Bridgeman Art Library
90–91	Turin, Galeria d'Arte Moderna

92–93 Potter Palmer Collection, 1922.414 © 1987 The Art Institute of Chicago. All Rights Reserved
94 The Baltimore Museum: Gift of Mabel Garrison Siemonn, BMA 1960.57/© DACS 1988
96–97 Rijksmuseum Kröller-Müller, Otterlo
98 Paris, Louvre
100–1 The Metropolitan Museum of Art, New York
102 Paris, Louvre
102–3 Potter Palmer Collection, 1922.425 © 1987 The Art Institute of Chicago. All Rights Reserved
104 Paris, Musée Marmottan
105 Musée des Beaux Arts, Tournai
106 Private Collection
109 Purchase from the Walter Aitken Fund Income, Major Acquisitions Centennial Fund Income, Martha E Leverone Fund, and Restricted Gifts of Friends of AIC in honor of Mrs Leigh B Block Committee on Major Acquisitions, 1970.98 © 1987 The Art Institute of Chicago. All Rights Reserved/DACS 1988
110 The Metropolitan Museum of Art, New York
111 Paris, Musée d'Orsay
113 Wadsworth Atheneum, Hartford. In memory of William Arnold Healy, given by his daughter Susie Healy Camp
114–5 Goteborgs Konstmuseum, Gotaplatsen
116–7 Goteborgs Konstmuseum, Gotaplatsen
118 National Gallery of Scotland
118–9 Musée d'Orsay, Paris/Cliché Musées Nationaux
120 National Gallery of Art, Washington DC
122 Giraudon/Musée d'Orsay, Paris/© DACS 1988
123 Museo Albi
124 Paris, Louvre/© DACS 1988
125 The Tate Gallery, London
127 Kunsthaus, Zurich
128 The Philadelphia Museum of Art
129 The Tate Gallery, London
130 Rijksmuseum Vincent Van Gogh, Amsterdam
131 Rijksmuseum Kröller-Müller, Otterlo
132–3 Rijksmuseum Kröller-Müller, Otterlo
134 Musée d'Orsay, Paris
137 Rijksmuseum Kröller-Müller, Otterlo
138–9 The Tate Gallery, London/© DACS 1988
141 Musée Fabre, Montpellier
142–3 The Metropolitan Museum of Art, New York
144 Collection Signac, Paris
145 Private Collection
146 Giraudon/Paris, Musée National d'Art Moderne/© DACS 1988
147 H Rupf Foundation,Kunstmuseum Bern
148 Paris, Musée National d'Art Moderne
149 Nationalmuseum, Moderna Museet, Stockholm/© DACS 1988
150–1 Paris, Collection Dott. Rondinesco
152 Kunstmuseum Basel
154 left Roger-Viollet/© DACS 1988
154 right Roger-Viollet
155 Roger-Viollet
156 Collection Niarches, Paris/Roger-Viollet
157 left Galerie Historique deVersailles/Roger-Viollet
157 right Musée Municipal, Arras/Giraudon
158 left Roger-Viollet
158 right Roger-Viollet
159 left Musée Derain, Chambourcy/Giraudon/© ADAGP, Paris and DACS, London 1988
159 right Paris, Musée Carnavalet/Giraudon
160 Collection Dufy/Giraudon/© DACS 1988
161 Art Institute of San Antonio/Giraudon
162 Roger-Viollet
163 Roger-Viollet
164 Roger-Viollet
165 Roger-Viollet
166 Roger-Viollet
167 Roger-Viollet
168 left Paris, Bibliotheque Nationale/Giraudon
168 right Roger-Viollet
169 Roger-Viollet
170 left Giraudon/© DACS 1988
170 right Paris, Musée National d'Art Moderne/Giraudon/© DACS 1988
171 Giraudon/© DACS 1988